D1042043

THE
MAKING
OF A
STAND-UP
GUY

CHARLIE MURPHY

with **Chris Millis**

THE
MAKING
OF A
STAND-UP
GUY

SIMON SPOTLIGHT ENTERTAINMENT

NEW YORK   LONDON   TORONTO   SYDNEY

SSE

Simon Spotlight Entertainment
A Division of Simon & Schuster, Inc.
1230 Avenue of the Americas
New York, NY 10020

First Simon Spotlight Entertainment hardcover edition December 2009

SIMON SPOTLIGHT ENTERTAINMENT and colophon
are trademarks of Simon & Schuster, Inc.

All photographs in this book except for the photo on page 126
have been provided courtesy of the author.

For information about special discounts for bulk purchases,
please contact Simon & Schuster Special Sales at 1-866-506-1949
or business@simonandschuster.com

The Simon & Schuster Speakers Bureau can bring authors to your live event.
For more information or to book an event contact the
Simon & Schuster Speakers Bureau at 1-866-248-3049
or visit our website at www.simonspeakers.com.

Designed by Jaime Putorti

Manufactured in the United States of America

1   3   5   7   9   10   8   6   4   2

Library of Congress Cataloging-in-Publication Data

Murphy, Charlie, 1959–
The making of a stand-up guy / by Charlie Murphy With Chris Millis.
p.   cm.
1. Murphy, Charlie, 1959–   2. Actors—United States—Biography.
3. Comedians—United States—Biography.   I. Millis, Chris.   II. Title.
PN2287.M8148A3   2009
791.450'28092—dc22   2009028598
[B]
ISBN 978-1-4391-2314-0
ISBN 978-1-4391-5053-5 (ebook)

In memory of both my biological father,
Charles Edward Murphy,
and my other father, the man who raised me,
Vernon Lynch, Sr.

Anyone who has given up will
never know just how close they
came to winning the game . . .

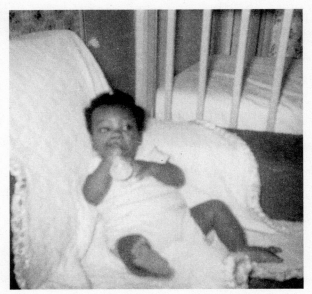

Here I am at six months old, drinking a protein shake.

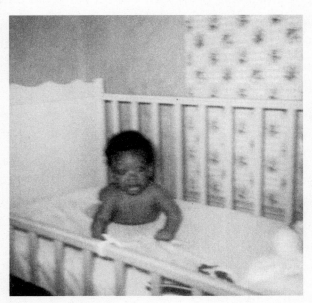

Me doing push-ups!

"CHECK IT OUT . . ."

I didn't take the stage as a stand-up comic until I was forty-two years old. Before that, I ran with a street gang, did time in jail, served in the military, managed a rap group, sold screenplays to Hollywood for hundreds of thousands of dollars, and traveled the globe as head of security for one of the most famous comedians and box office stars ever—my younger brother, Eddie Murphy.

But chances are you probably know me best as the dude who told those True Hollywood Stories about Rick James and Prince on Comedy Central's breakout sketch comedy hit *Chappelle's Show*. If you know my name at all, you probably know it as one long word, screamed at the top of your voice:

"CharlieMurphaaay!"

Through Dave Chappelle's brilliant characterization of Rick

James, my name became synonymous with Rick's larger-than-life persona and legendary party lifestyle. It was also an introduction for audiences to the lesser-known tales of our scraps over the years. After those segments exploded in popularity during the second season of *Chappelle's Show,* I found myself in the very strange position of suddenly having college kids approach me on the street and scream, in the voice of Rick James, "Hey, Charlie, what'd the five fingers say to the face?!"

Or, "Hey, Charlie . . . Fuck yo' couch, nigga!"

"They shoulda never gave you niggers money! I'm Rick James, bitch!"

Fuck yo' couch. For some folks, that's the same as walking up to me and saying hello.

I remember this dude came up to me once and yelled, "CharlieMurphaaay!"

I said, "Hey, man. How you doin'? What's goin' on?"

He said, "Charlie, I'm a big fan. I watched every episode of *Chappelle's Show.* Season one. Season two. Season three: The Lost Episodes. I'm a huge fan. I'd just like to say, Charlie, it would be an honor—matter of fact—"

The dude turned to his wife . . .

"Bitch, pull out your tits. Show Charlie Murphy your tits."

She did.

"Sign them titties, Charlie Murphy."

I autographed them.

The dude said, "Those are some nice titties. Ain't them nice titties, Charlie?"

"Not bad," I said. "Far as titties go."

"Charlie, it would be an honor if you'd come home with us and make love to my wife."

"It'd be an honor, huh?"

"Yes, Charlie Murphy. An honor."

"I appreciate the love, bro, but I'm gonna have to decline that most generous of offers."

In order to steer clear of trouble in these new situations, I had to learn to ask myself, *What would Rick James do?* Then, if I knew what was good for me, I would just do the opposite.

Despite its premature exit from the airwaves, and the strange circumstances surrounding its departure, *Chappelle's Show* remains an adored and relevant contribution to sketch comedy. When it was released on DVD, it instantly became the best-selling DVD of a television show ever. I've had lots of fun enjoying the fame that resulted from my appearances on the show, and the recognition I now receive as a successful headliner on the stand-up comedy circuit, but my life to this point has been far from the plot of some wacky sitcom.

From the early 1980s until just recently, I was accustomed to being known simply as Eddie Murphy's brother. And when my own breakout fame finally arrived in 2004, it was in a form that would forever link me to another American icon—Rick James. That's why, ultimately, I knew I had to find my own voice. To truly connect with audiences in a lasting and meaningful way, I had to discover something that was *all mine*.

That's how I came to stand-up comedy in my forties, more than twenty-five years after my brother wore the crown as the greatest stand-up comic in the world—arguably, of all time.

I may have arrived late to the party, but once I fell in love with the art of stand-up, I knew I had to take my act on the road and never, ever stop.

In the process of writing this memoir, I've uncovered a number of critical moments at which my life was irreversibly set on a new course. For instance, there was the night in Roosevelt, Long Island, when my ninth-grade classmate pressed a pistol to my forehead, with every intention of killing me, and pulled the trigger.

The round misfired.

That's why I'm still here today, able to share the many stories that have unfolded since that moment.

If I had died that night, I would've missed some seriously cool shit.

But I put myself in some tough situations growing up. It was the life I chose. And I know that today, too many young black men are still dying from violence. They aren't lucky enough to get the second chance I received.

I'm here to tell everybody that there's a lot of living to do in this world. It's worth it to make good decisions, do whatever you need to do to avoid those life-and-death situations, and live your life to the fullest.

Beyond that crucial encounter in Roosevelt, I can point to several other moments when my life changed direction, shaping me into the man I am today, including the murder of my father when I was ten years old; the galactic explosion of Eddie's career; receiving the gift of a crucial piece of advice from a seasoned stand-up comedian in my most desperate hour; and, of course, my breakout sketches on *Chappelle's Show*, which gave me the opportunity to discover that, away from the long shadow of my talented brother, I, too, had the ability to make people laugh.

Here's me performing at one of my earlier stand-up gigs.

CHAPTER ONE

THE LAUGH FACTORY

I began my stand-up career sitting down.

In the winter of 2004, as I took the stage of the Laugh Factory on Forty-second Street in Times Square for my very first performance as a stand-up comedian, I couldn't even make eye contact with the audience. It was about ten o'clock on a Thursday night during an open mic hosted by Rob Stapleton, and the house was packed with an all-black audience.

I knew what they were thinking.

What makes this guy think he can suddenly show up, twenty-five years after Eddie Murphy got famous, tell a joke, and make me laugh? Impossible.

I wasn't there to argue with them.

But that night in the Laugh Factory was another step along my path to better understanding who I was as an individual, of discovering what innate talents I possessed—away from the spotlight on my world-famous brother. Part of me was taking the stage that night to prove to myself that I wasn't afraid of performing live. But another part of me was extremely curious to find out if I could stand before a crowd, tell a story, and hear laughter in response. When I climbed onstage, I had no clue what was going to happen. I had no material. I had no idea how to structure a joke, let alone a ten-minute comedy set. I grabbed the mic, immediately sat down in a chair, and stared at my shoes. My mind was blank. I was scared shitless.

I thought, *How the fuck did I get here?*

One week earlier I was on the radio with the comedian TALENT, one of the hosts of *The Kiss 98.7 WakeUp Club* in New York City. I was in the studio with my friend and costar from *Chappelle's Show* Donnell Rawlings (Ashy Larry), talking about the instant popularity of the True Hollywood Stories sketches, which had recently premiered on Comedy Central.

TALENT said, "Charlie, the door is wide open now for you to do stand-up comedy."

"No," I said. "I don't really consider myself a stand-up comic. And I wouldn't want to disrespect the art form by going to clubs just to play off the buzz from these Rick James sketches. I don't think that'd be fair to all those comedians who work hard at their craft."

"What people don't realize about Charlie Murphy," Donnell said to TALENT, "is that they think he's some tough dude, like Tyree from the Mad Real World sketch on *Chappelle's Show*, or Gusto from *CB4*, or Jimmy from *Harlem Nights*. But really, Charlie's afraid to get in front of a microphone in a room full of people."

Everybody in the studio started laughing. They thought that was hilarious.

"The truth is," Donnell continued, "Charlie can talk on the radio or act in front of a camera, but if you put him up onstage in a club, he'll freeze up."

I took exception to what Donnell was saying. I had no problem standing in front of people, expressing myself.

I said, "The truth is, Donnell, I just don't consider myself a comedian."

"You're a comedian," said Donnell. "A comedian who's afraid to get on the mic."

I'll be the first to admit: I'm a dude who likes making people laugh, but I can't handle the feeling of being mocked and laughed at. And here I was, getting laughed at live on the radio, while Donnell called me out like I was some no-comedy bitch.

That night I turned over in my mind what Donnell had said. Why didn't I try stand-up comedy? Was I really not interested in it, or was it deeper than that? Was I afraid to fail publicly—

especially in an arena that my brother had mastered with such astronomical success?

I did some soul-searching and, a week after that radio interview with Donnell, I made up my mind.

I called Neal Brennan at three o'clock in the morning. Neal was the cocreator of *Chappelle's Show*. He's a comedian, writer, director, and all-around laid-back modern-day hippie dude. Neal had also directed and helped me write all my True Hollywood Stories segments. While I was on *Chappelle's Show*, I would often call Neal at odd hours whenever inspiration struck. He never seemed to notice what time of day or night I was calling.

I said, "Neal, I want to perform some stand-up comedy."

Neal thought about it for a long hippie minute. "You serious?"

"Yeah."

"Okay, Charlie. I'll call you back later with a time and place."

I didn't know it, but Neal decided to also call Donnell and invite him to meet us later that night at the Laugh Factory. Donnell was the last guy I wanted to see in the audience for my first stand-up performance. I don't handle failure well (as you'll learn later), and I knew Donnell would revel in it if I bombed. I'd never hear the end of it.

I drove into the city from New Jersey in my black Hummer, all decked out in diamond chains, gold jewelry, fancy clothes, and a big, expensive watch. I knew that most comedians struggle to make ends meet, so I was trying to give the impression that I was comfortable in my skin and had found success doing my thing. I was thinking I'd convince the audience that I was already a star. In reality, I was trying to mask the fact that when it came to taking the stage as a stand-up comic, on the inside I was like a scared little boy. When I entered the club, Neal and Donnell were waiting for me.

Donnell smiled. He said, "You're really going up there, huh?"

"Watch me," I said, with false bravado.

The Laugh Factory building on Forty-second Street used to house a peep show. It's a large venue with two bars and four or five big rooms on the upper level. While a show is in progress in one of the large rooms, the other comedians hang together in the greenroom. That night was my first time experiencing the camaraderie of being with other comedians as one of them— even if it was my first, and possibly final, public performance.

My first order of business was to toss back a couple glasses of chilled tequila. That was a mistake I would make before each performance for the next few years, having convinced myself that the looseness a buzz provided was a benefit to my stage act. Eventually I would learn that the alcohol created a silly, clownish stage presence and a false sense of confidence. But I was years away from those sorts of realizations, and for that moment, the booze helped to steel my nerves.

Before I took the stage, Neal said to me, "Charlie, whatever you do, don't try to be funny. Just be yourself."

The best thing I had going for me that night—the only thing, really—was that the True Hollywood Stories sketches had premiered the week before and were instantly popular with viewers. At the very least, people knew I was Eddie Murphy's brother. But that was as far as it went. No one had ever heard of me doing stand-up comedy.

So there I was, onstage, sitting in a chair, mind blank, avoiding making eye contact with the audience. Just me and the microphone.

Then, in a ridiculously transparent attempt to shield myself from potential failure and embarrassment, I uttered my first words as a stand-up comedian: "Look, I know you're all looking at me thinking, *What the fuck does Charlie Murphy think he's doing?* Well, all I can say about that is: Fuck y'all. I don't give a fuck if you motherfuckers laugh or not."

After I said that, the weirdest thing happened: People laughed.

I didn't realize it at the time, but with those words, I had inadvertently stumbled upon one of the golden rules of comedy: Always Address the Obvious.

I thought I was going to feel relieved to have gotten a laugh, but instead I felt something else entirely: fear. I was afraid I wasn't going to be able to figure out how to get that laughter back. I liked the sound of it, I liked the way it made me feel, and I was hungry for more. I had the odd sensation that I was holding the end of a rope, and each time I got a laugh, I felt another tug, pulling me along, farther and deeper into unexplored territory.

Everyone was having a good time laughing at my stories,

which I told in what basically amounted to a painfully shy stream-of-consciousness, cloaked in a nonchalant machismo. I talked to the audience like I normally talk, sitting there in a chair like some hip-hop version of Bill Cosby. They thought I had a routine, that I was doing bits. But I didn't know what the fuck I was doing. I was just shooting the shit. I was supposed to be on-stage for between five and ten minutes. I did fifteen.

I walked off to a round of applause, went to the bar, exhaled, and tossed back a few more tequilas. I was feeling a rush similar to the one I'd experienced the first time I'd gone skydiving. Sky-diving is one of those things where, for the longest time, you say, "I'm way too scared to try that. No way." Then one day you muster the courage to take the risk and find yourself up in a plane, strapped to some dude. Next thing you know, you're falling through the air, thinking, *Holy shit! I'm fucking skydiving! I might die!*

But I didn't die—not skydiving, and not onstage that night. I was terrified while it was happening, but it was a fun experience and I landed safely. To extend the metaphor a bit, I will say that comedy is a *lot* like skydiving in that the setup for each joke is like jumping from a plane, and the punch line is the parachute.

It would take years for me to professionally develop as a technique what I had just accidentally accomplished in those awkward first fifteen minutes on the stage of the Laugh Factory.

Rob Stapleton, who I had known for years, took the mic right after me. He wondered aloud to the audience why they were laughing. He told them I didn't have a set, that I had basically subjected them all to my psychiatry session. He said to the audience, "What's so funny? That's the same way that motherfucker talks in the car."

But they didn't care, and to me the entire evening felt like a great success. After the show Rob said, "Charlie, what you did tonight, that's what every comedian is searching for—a way to connect with the audience. The key is to figure out how to re-create that magic on a consistent basis. I hope you decide to stick with it because once you start doing stand-up, you can never stop. You've gotta keep pushing forward. Because if you stop, it's damn near impossible to start over again."

But I was barely listening. I had survived my first stand-up set, and all I wanted to do was drive home and collapse into my bed.

The next night the phone rang and it was Neal and Donnell. Neal said, "C'mon, you're going back out."

I said, "No. I'll probably go out again in, like, a week."

In my heart, I felt that what had happened the previous night at the Laugh Factory had been a wonderful stroke of luck, and I didn't want to tempt fate. I had no interest in heading right back out and jumping through rings of fire until I got burned.

"You can't wait till next week, Charlie," said Neal. "You have to strike while the iron is hot."

They convinced me to go out with them on a circuit of comedy clubs all over New York City—another set at the Laugh Factory, in addition to sets at the Comic Strip, Stand Up New York, the Comedy Cellar, and Gotham. The whole night was exhausting and terrifying. Plus, I think I knew what they were doing: They were dragging me to perform at every place they could think of until they saw me bomb. But I didn't bomb. People kept laughing at my non-act.

"This isn't supposed to be happening," grumbled Donnell. "Let's go to another club."

As the night wore on, I started getting more comfortable with the material I was delivering, and I started playing off the vibes I was feeling from the different audiences. I had cast away the chair and was now standing up, meeting their eyes (sometimes). I was getting addicted to the laughter—but, more than that, to the attention and the energy—and I wanted more.

I recognized that there was a lot more than just laughter going on while I was onstage. I needed to learn how to be comfortable in the spaces in between the jokes. I had to establish a rhythm with the audience and bring them along with me, up and down, like the Cyclone on Coney Island. Each time I took the stage, I was getting a little better, by tiny increments. I recognized immediately that each performance is a complete experience with its own beginning, middle, and end. It's a conversation, a spiritual connection, for a moment, with a roomful of people. Then that moment passes and all that's left are the good feelings and positive energy created from that interaction. Realizing this so early on freed me up to feel the love I was receiving from the audience, rather than being overcritical of myself or hyperaware that I didn't have the slightest clue what the fuck I was doing. I think a big part of why I succeeded in front of audiences right off the bat was because I gave myself permission to have fun.

Eight days later I was onstage in Old Westbury with Dave Chappelle, doing fifteen minutes of stand-up in front of a crowd of 5,500 people. At that point, I wasn't doing very much original comedy. All audiences wanted from me was a recap of the material they loved so much from the Rick James sketches. But even though I was merely feeding them what they already knew and were hungry to hear, word for word from the television segments, I was simultaneously developing my skills in timing, structure, and delivery to live—and sometimes extremely unruly—audiences. The enthusiasm and response I was receiving felt tremendous.

The laughter was seeping into my blood.

Stand-up comedy became my new passion. I was falling in love with the culture of comedy, and with the New York comedy scene. For the next month I performed in four or five clubs a night. When the first month was over, I had built up my first official ten minutes of stand-up material. I had jokes! Shit, I had a set!

Then, out of nowhere, I got a call from comedian Paul Mooney. Paul used to open for Richard Pryor, and later for Eddie, and he was also a writer and cast member in some of the most hilarious sketches on *Chappelle's Show*—such as Ask a Black Dude, Mooney on Movies, and Negrodamus.

Paul said, "I hear you're doing stand-up. I'm doing eight shows at Carolines this weekend and I want you to emcee."

"Are you serious?"

"Sure. You don't have to be that funny, and it's a chance to test out your jokes on a highly intelligent audience. Intelligent, because they'll all be there to see me."

"Yeah, Paul. I got it."

The gig at Carolines went great. Paul and many other comedians encouraged me to continue to work hard at my stand-up and refine my act.

Soon after my gig at Carolines, my cousin Rich, who is also my manager, came to me with plans for the "I'm Rich Bitch" comedy tour featuring me, Donnell, and fellow *Chappelle's Show* alum Bill Burr. Donnell and Bill had years of experience performing stand-up, and hours of material. I had twelve (pretty good, but by no means terrific) minutes of stand-up comedy, and now I was headed out on the road.

What was supposed to be a three-month tour turned into

nine months. When we started, we were getting ten thousand dollars a weekend and splitting it three ways. I was happy with that. Then, one day on the road, as the venues, crowds, and money continued to grow, Bill Burr said to me, "You realize, Charlie, that every time we do a show, it's sold out?"

"Yeah. Why? Is that not normal?"

"It's extremely *not normal*."

All I knew was that I was performing with two outstanding comedians—both pros with great sets—so I thought it was natural for us to enjoy so much success together.

Pretty soon, my twelve minutes grew to twenty, then thirty-five. I didn't realize it at the time, but as the months rolled past, I was gaining in popularity and stature, and all the while my material was improving.

Meanwhile, the True Hollywood Stories sketches were being constantly rerun on Comedy Central and had gone viral on the Internet. The segments, and the catchphrases that emerged from them, were becoming a phenomenon. Six months into the "I'm Rich Bitch" tour, I was stunned to learn that my name had become the main draw for audiences. When I had written forty-five minutes of stand-up material, I thought I had enough to try headlining my own show.

Donnell said, "Charlie, you've only been doing comedy for one year! Now you want to headline? You must be outta your goddamn mind."

Maybe so, but that didn't change the fact that I was determined to do it. Did I have forty-five minutes of quality stand-up?

Absolutely not. I was learning on the fly and enjoying success before I really even had a solid act. That was the powerful benefit of the crossover audiences I was attracting as a direct result of my popularity from *Chappelle's Show*. Even though my name recognition from television, DVD sales, and the Internet could fill the seats, I knew that I still had to come out with great material, entertain the audience, and make them feel like they got their money's worth. Most comedians pay their dues for a decade or more before acquiring the depth of material and confidence to consider themselves headliners. But I had a head of steam and I wasn't afraid anymore to perform live—on the contrary, I was thrilled by the challenge and plotting my next move.

That doesn't mean that, each step forward, I didn't still feel nervous and uncertain, but I resolved to power on through sheer tenacity. I still had a lot to prove to people who thought I was nothing more than just some one-hit brother of a famous person. I may not have had the most top-notch material yet, but what I did have was focus and a fierce desire to improve each time I stepped to the microphone.

My material slowly improved. One ringing endorsement came while I was on the road, from a dude who shit his pants laughing during one of my shows. One of the things people don't think about at live shows is that folks in the audience can have physical problems resulting from laughing too hard. When Eddie was at the top of his game, I saw people at his shows suffer heart attacks and hyperventilate and require oxygen. I even saw women going into labor—their water breaking right there in their seats. They all had to be rushed to the hospital straight from the show—from laughing too hard.

But through all that, I'd never seen anybody shit himself. I must've been on that night because when I make a man laugh so hard he soils his drawers, that's high praise indeed. The only reason I even found out it happened was because the staff at the club got into a fight with the dude when he refused to leave. He was having such a good time, he tried to act like it wasn't him. It's one thing to pretend it ain't you when you sneak out a fart, but when you've shit your pants, after a few minutes, it's confirmed, motherfucker. We all know it's you.

When the "I'm Rich Bitch" tour ended, comedian Mike Epps hired me to open for him on an eighteen-city tour. After our first few shows together, I started noticing a distinct difference between Mike's core audience and the folks who came out specifically to see me, still based mainly on the strength of my popularity from *Chappelle's Show*. Mike's audience was a hundred percent black; mine was mixed. Usually, there's a different energy in the room and a different approach for a black comedian to take when he's performing for an all-black crowd. There are certain protocols you've got to go along with, certain things that are expected of you by the audience, and if you don't follow those unspoken rules nobody has a good time. I didn't know that back then, so, like most things in my life, I had to learn this lesson the hard way.

Part of my problem was the attitude I was taking toward the audience. When I started opening for Mike, I went straight out and bought special clothes, complete with fancy sunglasses, and I was always dripping in diamonds and flashy jewelry. I remember looking at my reflection for, like, an hour before each show. I had a very low haircut at the time, called a Caesar, that I just kept brushing and brushing in front of the mirror. I said stuff to myself like, *You're gonna kill tonight.* I imagined the audience yelling and screaming, *We love you, Charlie!* All that psychosis was really going on inside my head. I strutted around all cocky backstage. I didn't pray before taking the stage. I was extremely proud of myself, even though I hadn't accomplished very much as a comedian up to that point. And I was drinking, too, trying to embolden my performance with the false sense of confidence alcohol provided.

One big mistake I made before opening for Mike Epps in St. Louis, Missouri, was to give an interview to the local newspaper in which I was so pumped up I said crazy shit like, "I'm the LeBron James of comedy. I'm bomb-proof. My skills are impeccable. I'm like Mike Tyson. . . ."

And I wasn't just saying that shit, either—I believed it.

The night that interview ran, I walked onstage wearing my expensive new shades and shiny suit and felt an instant clash in energy between the audience and myself. Something was amiss from the get-go. I grabbed the microphone and said about three words before voices in the crowd started booing. It took me a moment to figure out what was happening; I'd never been booed before. There were about 4,500 people in the venue, and suddenly most of them were booing me at the top of their lungs. An unfamiliar wave of churning nausea washed over me. I was in completely uncharted territory. I had been on a nonstop winning streak for nearly two years, receiving nothing but love from every audience. Eventually, it dawned on me: *Holy shit. I'm bombing.*

All the way at the back of the room, I heard a little voice squeak out, "You ain't Eddie."

I'll never forget that voice. When I heard it, I thought, *Is that what these people think? That I'm trying to be Eddie Murphy? Wow. They have me all wrong.*

I wasn't trying to be my brother—I was trying to show people what *I* had to say. So my defenses kicked in.

I said, "Well, being as how you don't want to hear what I have to say, there's only one thing left for me to tell you: Fuck you. Fuck all of you country-assed, gold-toothed, backwoods motherfuckers."

It was the same tough-guy front I had thrown up to protect myself from embarrassment during my very first performance, at the Laugh Factory. Except back then, my words were expressed out of a genuine humility and a profound fear of failure. On the stage that night in St. Louis, my words were coming from an attitude of anger and entitlement.

And no one was laughing.

After I told the audience to go fuck themselves, they went absolutely bananas. They howled and carried on like I was stabbing them in their throats. People leapt up and screamed, "Fuck you, Charlie Murphy! Get that motherfucker outta here!"

For a while I stood my ground, refusing to be run offstage. I wanted to leave on my own terms. I waited for an opportunity, then I said, "I just want everybody here to know, since this is our first—and probably last—time meeting face-to-face, FUCK YOU, TOO! I got your money. I'm going to get a lap dance."

Then I dropped the mic and walked offstage.

What a fucking disaster.

Backstage, I stalked around, drinking tequila and feeling like a real asshole. In retrospect, I don't hold any of that night against the audience; I hold it against myself. I acted out because my feelings were hurt. In truth, I was crushed. The whole thing happened the way it did because of my inexperience, my immaturity as a performer, and my ego.

Back in my hotel room, I was feeling pretty sorry for myself, so, at three o'clock in the morning, I called Eddie.

He said, "Whaddya want?"

"Yo. I can't believe what just happened, man."

"What happened?"

"I got booed off the stage. By forty-five hundred people."

"Really?"

"Yeah."

"So . . . Who do you think you are?"

"What?"

"You heard what I said. Who do you think you are?"

"I don't understand what you're saying."

"Well, Richard Pryor got booed off the stage. Bill Cosby got booed off the stage. Martin Lawrence got booed off the stage. Chris Rock got booed off the stage. Bernie Mac got booed off the stage. I got booed off the stage. You name him, Charlie, and he's been booed off the stage. So now I'm asking you: Who the fuck do you think you are, Charlie Murphy?"

I didn't know what to say.

Eddie said, "Look, man, don't be calling me no more this late about some bullshit."

And he hung up the phone.

I sat there in that hotel room in St. Louis with the phone to my ear for probably another five minutes, just listening to the dial tone. My brother had just given me an intellectual ass-kicking. It was harsh, but it was real. I knew that what he was saying to me in that moment was true, but I didn't want to accept it. It was all part of my education as a stand-up. The reality is, you're not a real comedian until you bomb. That was my first time experiencing that reality—and it sucked.

But it would take at least one more solid kick in the nuts for that lesson to start sinking in.

The next show was in Cleveland. I had recovered psychologically (sort of), convincing myself that the St. Louis show had been a freak thing, an aberration, so I was back to the old me: flashy sunglasses, dripping in diamonds, staring in the mirror—a rock star. It was the same bush league shit all over again. I strutted out onto the stage in front of that Cleveland audience and . . .

It happened again. They booed me right off.

That show was the wake-up call, the experience that finally shook me from my stupor. I realized in that moment that I had lost my focus and overdone it with my shiny clothes and my giant ego. I was trying to look the part of a star, even though I was far from becoming one yet. I had come a long way from those first moments at the Laugh Factory, sitting in a chair and avoiding eye contact, but somewhere along the road I had lost sight of my first responsibility as a comedian: Make a connection with the audience. As a result, all I looked like when I stepped to the mic was a big fraud.

I decided to sit down with Mike Epps. I said, "Hey, man. I respect the fact that you gave me an opportunity to be a part of your show, but it's not working out. The crowd is booing me. I don't want people who are coming to see you and have a good time have this be part of their experience. They shouldn't be booing anything. Everybody should be happy and having fun. So I'm gonna quit."

Mike said, "Don't quit, Charlie. I know how you feel; it's happened to me before. It happens to all good comedians. Nigger, look—you can do this. You're a funny brother. Don't quit."

I was quiet for a minute and finally said, "Okay."

I mean, what else could I say?

• • •

After bombing in St. Louis and Cleveland, we rolled up to our next show at Constitution Hall in Washington, D.C. By that time, all sorts of crazy, negative thoughts were swirling inside my mind. This was the very same venue where Eddie had performed his breakout stand-up triumph, *Delirious*, in 1983. Suddenly I was terrified all over again about standing in front of a live audience.

As the car approached the venue, I looked out at the sold-out crowd of 3,702 people climbing the steps into the performance hall. My palms were slick with sweat. My heart kept throwing itself against the inside of my chest like it was trying to bust down a door.

I turned to my cousin Rich and said, "This is it. I'm gonna die here tonight. If I bomb tonight like I bombed the last two nights, it's over for me, man. I quit."

I made up my mind that bombing in Constitution Hall would be all the proof I needed to know I wasn't the real deal; to know, once and for all, that I wasn't a professional stand-up comedian, and that I was never going to be one.

As soon as I got inside the venue, I was told that a very famous stand-up comedian was waiting for me inside my dressing room. I didn't want to talk with anyone, especially since I was sick with the feeling that I was about to bomb for the third straight performance and that my career as a stand-up was all but over. When they told me who was waiting to speak with me, I thought, *What does that brother want?*

I was horrified.

As it happened, all that brother wanted was to say hello and to pass along to me a crucial piece of advice that would change my whole approach to stand-up comedy from that point forward, teaching me how to ingratiate myself to an audience, and saving my career in the process.

But before I get into who that comedian was and what he had to tell me, allow me to introduce myself.

Me and Daddy coming home from a walk, 1962.

CHAPTER TWO

BROOKLYN, PART ONE
(MOM AND DAD)

Like I said, my life growing up was no sitcom. Even though our nicknames were Charlie Wally (me) and Slop McGopp (Eddie), we weren't jumping around the apartment like Steve Urkel and Arnold Drummond, making the family laugh all the time. It wasn't like our dad would walk in the house, queue the background music, and zing out a one-liner. We were a normal family who did normal family stuff. Eddie was interested in entertainment and pursued it. I, on the other hand, would travel down many avenues (most of them dead ends) before I discovered my true passions in life.

I was born Charles Quinton Murphy on July 12, 1959, in Elmhurst Hospital, Queens, to Charles Edward and Lillian Christine Murphy. Though I was born in Queens, I was there for only one day, so I claim Brooklyn as my home. My parents were married when they were nineteen years old and had two children: me and Edward Regan Murphy, born April 3, 1961.

As is the case with most Brooklyn families, money was tight in our house. Dad had a job as a deliveryman for a drugstore. That was his sole income, and that's how he was supporting the family. Dad was an amateur actor and comedian and would perform with his brothers. Many years earlier, my Grandma Rosa had gone to a soothsayer who told her that one of her offspring was going to be world-famous. It turned out that all of her sons—Ray, Sonny, LeRoy, James, and my father, Charles—became performers. They told jokes, they sang, and they danced. At our barbecues, all five of them would get up and perform in the backyard until they had everyone at the party eating out of the palms of their hands.

First we lived in the Tilden Projects in Brownsville, then in Williamsburg, then later on Linden Street in Bushwick. I've got a lot of good memories from those Brooklyn neighborhoods. All the people in the buildings were our friends, and I remember how everyone would gather together on weekends, play cards, cook, and hang out while all us kids would run off and play together.

One thing all the buildings in the neighborhood had in common was that no one had a washer and dryer in their apartment; they were always in the basement. Those basements were creepy, and there weren't any windows, so no one would ever hang around down there while their clothes were in the machines.

One day, us kids checked inside the dryer and found a big fishnet. Back then, people used to stretch those nets across their walls or ceilings for ornamentation in their homes. It was purely for decorative purposes—this was not a real net, like in the circus. But we didn't know that.

I said, "Y'know what we're gonna do? We're gonna make this into a trampoline."

We took the net upstairs in front of the building and strung it from one stoop to the next. When you're at the top of one of those brownstone stoops in Brooklyn, you're half a story above street level. Once we had the net secured around the railings, I declared that I was going to be the first to test it out. Then up stepped one of the neighborhood kids, Thomas Edwards. Thomas had a speech impediment, so he pronounced his name "TomaEdwa."

Thomas said, "No, no, Char, do na go fir. Imma go fir."

Thomas climbed up on the banister and yelled, "Dwon die," which translated to "Swan dive."

He dove off the edge, and when he hit that net, it was like nothing was there. He fell straight through to the pavement, smashing his face.

Thomas peeled his bloody face off the sidewalk and ran crying all the way home. These days, I'm often complimented on my bright, wide smile. I suppose I have TomaEdwa to thank for saving me from losing all my front teeth back in Brooklyn.

There was also a playground nearby where we'd go to run around, climb on the monkey bars, and swing on the swings. Inevitably, in the projects, you're going to bump into rough kids. I learned early on that I was rougher than most. It was like I'd been born with a reckless willingness to fight. This instinct first revealed itself in those playground days, down on the sandbox level. Back then, it wasn't like it is now, with all the parents sitting around watching their kids while they play a few feet away. There were never any parents around, so fights would break out fairly frequently. One day a girl kept pushing me around. Back then, the girls in the neighborhood could be bigger, meaner, and stronger than most of the boys. They were always testing limits to see what they could get away with. Once you were issued a beat-down on the street—from a boy or a girl—your respect quotient from the other kids plummeted.

So, I beat her up.

Her mother stormed over to our apartment and told my mom all about it. Mom didn't like the idea of me laying hands on little girls (she wasn't interested in the intricate power politics of the playground), so she spanked me and told me to leave the girls alone.

She said, "Charlie, don't you ever put your hands on another girl like that again."

I didn't. But as a result, the neighborhood girls soon learned that they could do whatever they wanted to me and I wouldn't hit back. They began a brutal campaign of hitting, slapping, and scratching me at every opportunity. This went on for a while—me coming home dirty and scratched up—until one day

Mom said, "Y'know what, Charlie? I'm tired of seeing you get whupped. It's time to start fighting back again."

I made quick work of the next girl who attacked me, and that was the end of that.

That was a short phase of my life, but when I reflect on it now, I think it left me permanently scarred with a lot of residual resentment against women. How could it not? Most of the first girls I ever knew in my formative years spent all their time and energy whipping my ass.

As far as our family dynamic goes, I was the older brother, so I always felt it was my responsibility to be the vanguard. That sense of responsibility still echoes in my mind and continues to shape me into the person I am today. I never had the luxury of being afraid of other people (no matter how big or nasty they were) or of running away from any situation. I had to stand up and protect my brother.

I encountered many a bully growing up in Brooklyn. It was on those streets that I learned I had the strength and courage to stand and fight. It was neighborhood justice, fast and brutal, but it was also my duty as the older brother. Everyone always knew that if my brother told somebody he was going to get Charlie, there was going to be trouble. There was never a time when Eddie came to fetch me where I arrived on the scene to have a rational discussion. By the time I arrived, all conversational avenues had been exhausted. When Charlie showed up, it was bombs away.

I maintain an element of that style of conflict resolution to this day. When a situation involves my kids or my nieces and nephews, I can still respond like Sonny Corleone: jumping into my car all pissed off, speeding toward the action without a plan. Turns out that's not always the way to handle things in life. Little by little, I've learned that it's best to step back from situations and calm myself down before I react.

Baby steps.

In the summers, I would spend all day at McCarren Park Pool in Greenpoint, Brooklyn. I would roll my swim trunks into my towel and pile onto the train in Bushwick with a crew of about a dozen kids and ride the four stops over to the park. We would each have twenty-five cents jingling in our pockets: ten cents to get into the pool and fifteen to spend on snacks. We combined all of our money and shared the different treats and drinks that we bought.

We would swim at McCarren Pool all . . . day . . . long. It was a giant community pool—originally designed to accommodate 6,800 swimmers—and the city would shock it so harshly that when we stepped off the train at the end of the day to walk home, all you could smell for a block and a half was chlorine. Our eyes looked like bing cherries, watery with tears from the burn of all those chemicals, but we didn't care. We couldn't get enough.

Eventually, we kids would gravitate back to the building from the playground or swimming pool toward the sounds of hysterical laughter. All the grown-ups would be huddled together, doubled over laughing as they listened to Redd Foxx's album *Live & Dirty, Volume 3*, or Richard Pryor's *Bicentennial Nigger*, or Rudy Ray Moore's *Dolemite*. Those albums were hilarious—and filthy, which fascinated me. These old-school dudes used profanity and talked about sex and bathroom humor. I couldn't believe they were allowed to talk like that on records you could buy at the store!

Redd Foxx would say, "People have said I'm dirty because I say 'fuck.' To me, the only time fuckin' is dirty is when you don't wash up after. I could say 'intercourse,' but if you're doing it right, you're fuckin'."

When we lived in the Tilden Projects, I remember my dad spanking me only one time.

In the projects, the apartments had what were called slam-shut windows—windows that opened out, then slammed shut when you closed them. We lived on the eighth or ninth floor, and one day I got it in my mind that I was going to climb through the slam-shut window and stand on the ledge of the building. I had one leg dangling outside and was just getting ready to throw the other one over the ledge when my father walked into the room and saw what I was doing. He was so frightened he snatched me back into the room and immediately gave me a smack on the ass. But that was the only time.

He was a laid-back guy, my dad. He didn't discipline me very harshly, or very often. He worked hard and didn't see us kids much, so when he was around, he preferred to be delighted by the trouble we got into. Whatever mischief I cooked up, Dad usually thought it was pretty funny. He liked to laugh. Of course, that made me think he was the coolest dad in the world.

I was a curious kid, always climbing over furniture and shelves or rooting around in drawers. If I was the only one in the apartment, I would search through every drawer and cupboard, under every bed and behind every door, getting into everybody's private business. My constant climbing and burrowing through drawers gave me the bright idea one morning to wake up before everyone else and pull down the Flintstone vitamins Mom gave to Eddie and me with breakfast every morning. That way, I could distribute as many Freds and Wilmas and Pebbles and Bamm-Bamms between us as we desired. The weird part was that the pills were all colored red, and they weren't formed in the shapes of all those lovable cartoon characters. Also, they weren't in a Flintstones vitamin container, but I happily disregarded all those warning signs as I doled the pills out to Eddie and myself. Fortunately, the bitter taste forced us to spit them out before we swallowed them because we learned later that they were Mom's birth control pills. I later thought it was strange that Mom even had those pills in the house because, as it turned out, she was not done having babies.

• • •

In 1965, when I was about six years old and Eddie was four or five, Mom and Dad divorced. We left the Tilden Projects and went to live across from my grandma Rathie on Linden Street—we were number seventeen, she was number eighteen. Mom had a younger brother, Keith, who lived with Grandma Rathie and was only four years older than me. He became like a big brother to Eddie and me and we would all pal around together, roaming the neighborhood like a real crew.

Dad moved into his own apartment. He eventually began dating a new woman, and he was hired as an officer for the New York City Transit Authority. Dad would come pick Eddie and me up and take us out during the day for different adventures around the city. Sometimes Mom would put us on the train at Gates Avenue and we would ride all alone to meet him at Broadway Junction.

When I think about that now, I'm amazed at the freedom we had as little kids in those days to wander around New York City. I would never allow my kids to do that today. If someone told me right now that my son, who's nine years old, was on the train alone with no adult, I would pull my hair out—and I'm bald-headed. I can't imagine my son just being out and about in the neighborhood, doing his own thing—let alone hopping subway trains and wandering the streets of New York—and me not even really wondering where he is or what he's into. It was a different world in the Brooklyn of the 1960s. Maybe it's just that parents are more aware these days of the perils out there. Maybe information isn't as suppressed for the sake of image as it was back then. Or maybe parents in those days just operated under a false sense of security, thinking their children would always be safe. I know I would have done whatever I needed to do to protect myself, but the fact is, it wasn't that I was safe and secure all those years, it's that I was damn lucky.

When we lived on Linden Street, Mom got a job as an operator for Bell Telephone and started working odd hours on a split shift. Grandma Rathie worked, too, so we had a series of babysitters. One was a young girl named Angie.

One day, after Mom left for work, a man came over who we'd never seen before. He took Angie into Mom's bedroom and closed the door. I thought, *Who's this man and what's he doin' in my momma's room?* I peeked under the door to see what they were doing. I heard belt buckles jingling, saw a bra and pants drop to the floor, and caught a glimpse of bare ankles. I had no idea what I was looking at. Later that night, Mom was giving me a bath before she put me to bed and I said, "Oh, yeah, by the way, a man came over today and changed Angie's diaper."

Needless to say: no more Angie.

After that, Mom called on a few close friends to watch us—Terra, Shirley, Gloria—but they had kids of their own, and maybe Mom started feeling guilty. So she decided to find somebody steady to drop us off with while she was at work during the day and, because of her split shift, sometimes overnight.

Mom made arrangements for us to start going over to the

house of a lady named Ms. Jenkins. The first time Mom took us there, Ms. Jenkins was very, very friendly. She smiled as she described to my mother how she ran her house. Ms. Jenkins handed me, Eddie, and Uncle Keith each a lollipop. Mom was satisfied, so she paid Ms. Jenkins and said she'd be back soon to pick us up. That's my first memory of being in someone's house who I didn't know. I kept thinking, *Who's this lady? I don't wanna stay here.*

As soon as she closed the door, Ms. Jenkins wheeled around, her face contorted in a cruel sneer, like some horror movie monster. She snatched away our lollipops and said, "Get in the other room." Then she twisted the wet lollipops back into their wrappers and placed them back in the bowl. That was our introduction to the real Ms. Jenkins. And she would only get meaner.

Ms. Jenkins wasn't just watching us; she had a whole house full of kids. There was a television in the living room—a great tool for any babysitter—but she never let us watch it. She would say, "I don't want you kids using up my TV," as if we could exhaust all the shows that were stored inside it.

She was abusive, too. When she thought we were misbehaving, she used to make us go outside and cut down a switch, which is a thin whip of a branch. Then she would peel off all the bark, down to the green, wet part, and use it to spank us. She beat us on a regular basis for the slightest infractions. Ms. Jenkins employed any tactic in her arsenal to scare us.

For instance, some of the other kids under her care suffered from eczema. Eczema is not contagious, but we didn't know that. All we saw were kids crying, with pus dripping out of their arms, constantly scratching the pink patches of calamine lotion dabbed all over their bodies.

When we were forced to stay the night, Ms. Jenkins would use that situation to threaten us. She would point to one of the kids with eczema and say, "You were bad; you're sleeping in bed with him tonight."

Or, if one of the little kids wet the bed, everybody sleeping in that bed would get whipped with a switch. How was it that everybody sleeping in the bed got whooped because one kid pissed? Ms. Jenkins never felt she needed to explain her logic to us.

Ms. Jenkins must have saved an impressive amount on her grocery bills, because she often would feed us a meal of lima beans, white rice, and pigtails, which look like tiny snakes and taste like toenails. She wouldn't let us leave the table until we cleaned our plates.

She used to fill the bathtub and then send in the first boy to wash himself. Then she'd send in the next, and the next—without ever emptying or refilling the tub. When everybody was done she'd make us stand in the middle of the living room to air dry. The girls would be sitting on the floor, laughing and pointing at our naked, shivering bodies. But they would be next.

Ms. Jenkins wasn't just a petty, cruel, and stingy daycare

provider; she was also a slumlord who rented apartments to local vagrants. At night, as I lay awake beside a feverish mound covered in calamine lotion, hoping he didn't piss himself, I would listen to bums snoring off their benders. Then, in the morning, we'd all watch them outside, shooting dope.

Years later Eddie appeared on *Inside the Actors Studio* with James Lipton. When Lipton asked Eddie about Ms. Jenkins, Eddie's face twisted into a sort of pained, polite smile as he tried to laugh it off, and then he did an impression of me.

Eddie replied, "My brother said, 'If I was walking down the street, and I seen Ms. Jenkins right now, I'd punch her in the face.' "

Eddie finished by coming to the same conclusion I had: "She was really mean, Ms. Jenkins."

Of course, I wouldn't really punch an old lady in the face. But a person like that deserves some lasting misery because she took advantage of little kids when we were helpless to defend ourselves.

In the end, Ms. Jenkins's tactics were finally discovered by my mom and Grandma Rathie when the buckle on a belt she was using to whip Uncle Keith caught him in the eye.

She was a crafty old bat, but there was no hiding that one.

• • •

All along, I still saw my father regularly. He was doing okay on his own, all things considered.

Then, in 1969, Eddie and I were playing outside when Mom came to the door and called us upstairs. She sat us both down in the living room and said, "Your father was killed last night."

We learned later from a cousin that Dad had been murdered by his girlfriend while he slept. The story went that they had an argument and she left the room. Dad suffered from narcolepsy, a condition that made him prone to suddenly falling asleep, regardless of the location or circumstances. At the time, the girlfriend's whole family was there in the house: mother, father, and brother.

My father sat down and instantly fell asleep. About twenty minutes later, she returned to the room and stabbed him in the heart.

And here's what happened to her: nothing.

She went to jail for one night. I can't explain why she did no time for my father's murder. That doesn't mean I don't understand why it probably went down that way. My father wasn't just a New York City Transit police officer, he was a *black* New York City Transit police officer, in the 1960s. The fact that he was a cop never entered into it. It was dubbed a lover's quarrel, a crime of passion.

My belief is that if you kill a cop, you kill a cop. It doesn't matter whether you're sticking up a Wendy's or you're upset because he's breaking up with you. But that's not how my father's case was handled.

Even though we were little kids, we instantly grasped the full weight and consequences of what our mother was telling us. But I was the tough guy, the older brother, and in that moment I believed I was now the man of the family. I cried for about ten minutes, then I stopped. I stopped because Eddie was crying so hard. I kept saying, "Don't cry, Eddie. Stop crying."

But he kept on crying—for a week, at least. I realized many years later that what Eddie was doing was the best way to handle the news of our father's murder. I didn't deal with it then, choosing instead to keep my emotions bottled up out of a sense of responsibility and, perhaps, what I considered at that tender age to be manliness. Dealing with the news of Dad's death the way I did, in that moment, has definitely had its lasting effects on me. I think I didn't cry enough. I didn't let out the pain or the anger or the grief. I held it all inside. No question, it damaged me.

The only thing worse than how I dealt with the news of my father's death was the funeral itself. Seeing him cold and lifeless inside his coffin was a fucking nightmare. There was my Superman, my daddy, only twenty-seven years old, dead in a box with everybody staring and sobbing.

I'll never forget standing alongside the coffin when some woman grabbed my hand and placed it on his body.

She said, "G'head. Touch him."

I resent that woman to this very day. That moment made the entire experience and lasting memory of my father's death much more morbid and surreal for me; much more awful. That was my daddy, the man whose lap I used to climb into, snuggle my face into the stubble on his neck, and fall asleep. Now that person, all those memories, felt like some wax replica stuffed in a box, and someone I didn't even know had forced my hand on him.

Then there was all the carrying on—the wailing and screaming, fainting in the aisles, shrieking out things that only the person who's screaming can possibly understand. I think all that shit people do at funerals is for their own selfish purposes. It certainly doesn't bring any comfort to the family. It only serves to make things worse for everyone else in attendance, all those people trying to show respect by grieving with dignity. I hated how people fell all over themselves at my father's funeral. It was a tragedy, but the circus atmosphere surrounding his service made it ten times worse.

The year my father passed, I dealt with death four times. The first funeral I ever attended was for a dude named Larry who I knew from the block. His mother had fifteen children and one night his building caught fire. She got fourteen kids out, but couldn't find the youngest daughter. Larry raced back into the building, where he died with his sister. A couple months later I was at Dad's funeral. A couple months after that, I was at the funeral of my father's mother, Grandma Rosa. And a couple months after that, I was at the funeral of my aunt. That was a rough fucking year for a ten-year-old.

Me and Mom, 1993.

Vernon Lynch, Sr. with the grandkids.
I miss you, Pop!

CHAPTER THREE

BROOKLYN, PART TWO
(MOM AND POP)

After Dad was gone, and with Grandma Rosa passing shortly after, it felt as if my world had shrunk to just Mom, me, Eddie, Grandma Rathie, and Uncle Keith. But we made it work. And a new development in the time before Dad's death was that Mom had begun seeing the man she would eventually marry, who would support our family, and who Eddie and I would grow to love as our father. His name was Vernon Lynch.

Mr. Lynch, who we eventually called Pop—reluctantly at first, then later with warm affection—is the man who gave me my sense of morality and principles. He's the only man I've ever met who was incapable of being untruthful. Pop had an iron integrity, no matter the situation or the consequences. He despised liars.

In his early days, Pop was a professional prizefighter, but he had retired by the time he met Mom. He liked to keep his head in the game, though, so he'd take me over to the gym near the merchant marine base in the Brooklyn Navy Yard. The toughest dude in the gym was a ropy teenager named Eddie Gregory. He became a Golden Gloves champion and, several years later, Eddie Gregory renamed himself Eddie Mustafa Muhammad. Several years after that, Eddie Mustafa Muhammad became the light heavyweight champion of the world.

The discipline of boxing was ingrained in Pop's personality. He didn't tolerate profanity or slang. He was a stickler for education and demanded that we study hard and apply ourselves at school. He taught us to respect our parents. Pop showed me how to be a decent person and how to conduct myself like a man. He led by example, but I didn't always follow.

What stood out about him the most, for me, was that back then a lot of black men wore big hats, platform shoes, shirts with psychedelic flower prints, and flared pants. Pop didn't wear any of that stuff. When I think about how everybody was dressing back then, I think of that shit as "clown clothes." But Pop was always buttoned-down, clean-cut, and straight up.

Soon after Mom married Pop, his sister moved across the street with her two kids, Bernard and Delores. So, with Uncle Keith, me, Eddie, and Bernard, we had a little crew that would prowl around the neighborhood. At the time, that neighborhood seemed so big to me, but now, when I go back, it's so small.

There was no Internet then, of course, and our parents weren't buying us a new toy every month, so we had to find things to keep us busy the old-fashioned way. I mean, if you got a spinning top as a gift, that was your toy for the whole year until it got cracked in a game or something. Or you'd make your own toys. We would find an old skate, break up a wooden box, and make a skateboard out of it. That's the kind of thing kids don't even contemplate today.

We would do anything to entertain ourselves. We would rip up a cardboard box to make shields, and then the kid with the biggest head would run around as the Rampaging Head, ramming his head into the cardboard, trying to knock us all down.

We'd make up all sorts of games using discarded boxes or cardboard shavings. One day when we were playing in a big box we looked at the building across the street and saw two men standing in the vestibule. Suddenly, one man ran away, leaving the other with a blooming flower in his hand.

We soon realized, though, that he wasn't holding a flower— he was holding a handkerchief soaked in his own blood. The other man had sliced his fingers and robbed him. We went over and helped the man upstairs to his apartment. He was grateful, so he sat us down and gave us cookies and milk. That made me feel like a good Samaritan, like I was doing the right thing, and it inspired me to want to always tell when I saw bad things happening in the neighborhood. But the code in the 'hood was "No snitching." That rule extended to everyone on the block—even

Pop, who felt that withholding information from the police to keep his children safe wasn't the same as telling a lie.

One day we were playing near a local factory and we watched these dudes looking around for where the inventory was kept. The next morning, as we headed to school, we watched those same dudes carting out wheelbarrows stacked high with sweaters from inside the factory. They'd been robbing the place all night.

After school, we were back playing in the same spot as before when the police came around. They asked us if we'd seen any strange men or activity in the past day. Because I had seen what good could come from doing the right thing after helping that man with the red flower in his hand, my intention was to tell the police the truth.

Up in the apartment, in front of Mom and Pop, I told the policeman everything I'd seen. When he left, my mother gave me one of the most tremendous ass-whippings of my life. I learned the lesson of the 'hood that day: No snitching. Mom's message was: If we wanted to live there comfortably, without Pop and her constantly worrying about our safety, we didn't run our mouths about what we saw in the street.

That may seem harsh, but we were living in the real world.

That lesson has stayed with me to this day. I'm not a police officer, nor do I consort with criminals, so I mind my own business. About the only thing that would force me to open my mouth would be if I saw something really heinous perpetrated in front of me—like someone harming a defenseless person. Outside of that, I don't spend any of my time running around, turning people in. I teach my kids that things happen in this world over which we have no power. I tell them to be wary of placing their full trust in people who aren't close friends and family. That's just how I was raised.

In those first years when Vernon Lynch was the new man in my mother's life—long before I dreamed of calling him anything as loving and respectful as Pop—I completely rejected his presence. At first, I was so angry about my parents' divorce, and later, about my Dad's death, that the idea of this new dude spending time with my mother was entirely unacceptable to me. I refused to call him Vernon, so I called him Herman instead.

I didn't want to follow his rules or listen to what he had to say. I challenged him every step of the way. It seemed our personalities were specifically designed to clash. On top of that, there was the constant struggle for my mother's attention. As a little boy, I thought there was no way I could ever lose the battle for my momma's heart and affection, but of course I was too young to understand all the complex emotions involved in the situation.

When I was thirteen, Mom and Pop caught me smoking cigarettes. Most of the adults around me smoked, and I wanted to act grown-up. The Marlboro Man smoked. John Wayne smoked. Those dudes were badasses.

When I finally managed to get my own pack of cigarettes, I hid them in my underwear drawer—the same drawer my mother went into every week to put away my laundry. A few days later, Mom called me into the bedroom. I knew something was up. She and Pop were waiting for me beside my open underwear drawer.

Mom said, "What's this?"

"Underwear."

Pop snatched up the cigarettes. "This."

"Well, these guys were having a smoke-ring-blowing contest at school. This dude, John, was afraid he'd get in trouble if his parents saw him bringing home cigarettes, so he gave them to me to hold on to."

Pop said, "A smoke-ring-blowing contest? At school?"

"Yeah."

"You really think I'm gonna stand here and buy your bull-shit?"

"I guess not."

It couldn't have been easy for Pop, raising somebody else's sons. He did a great job, but I tested him every step of the way. I fueled the tension between us. I guess in my own way I was try-ing to man up, but it was all for naught in the end because Mr. Lynch was a good dude. I was just one of those kids who was programmed to always buck against authority and reject new circumstances.

Pop worked the graveyard shift at the Breyers Ice Cream

factory, moving around skids on the factory floor and in the warehouse, eventually becoming foreman. He took me down there a few times and showed me the biggest refrigerator I've ever seen in my life. Because of the hours he worked, when we went to school Pop would be home sleeping, and when we got home he would be getting ready for work. That was perfect for Pop because if we had done anything to get into trouble that day at school, he had that little window of time to straighten us out. And he was fully rested.

One afternoon I was on the front stoop fixing a flat tire on my bicycle when some doped-up junkie wandered up to me. When we lived on Linden Street, we were only a block from Gates Avenue, which to this day is still one of the roughest areas in that section of New York. It was like night and day: Linden Street—nothing going on. Gates Avenue—drugs, prostitution, gambling, shootings, all kinds of trouble. Inevitably, every now and then, that shit would spill over onto our block.

So this junkie stumbled up to me and said, "What're you doin'? Fixing a tire on that bike?"

"Yeah."

"Fix it again."

"Whaddya mean, 'fix it again'?"

"I want you to fix it again."

I said, "I just fixed it."

"Fix it again."

Suddenly Pop appeared on the stoop. He said, "What do you want?"

"I want this boy to fix this tire again."

"Get outta here, fool."

The junkie straightened up. He said, "I ain't goin' nowhere till he fixes this tire."

Pop disappeared back inside the building. I thought he'd run off and left me. Next thing I knew, Pop stormed back out, waving the biggest kitchen knife we had in his hand. He chased that junkie right off the block.

In 1967, not long after Mom and Pop were married, Mom gave birth to a son, Vernon Lynch, Jr., who we called Vern. I wasn't excited to learn that I now had to share a bedroom not only with Eddie but also with a new brother who was eight years younger than me.

Vern quickly became my new science project. As we grew together, Vern didn't know any better, so he unwittingly looked up to me as an authority figure, even though I was barely any smarter than him. Poor Vern would do just about anything I told him to do. We would watch TV shows like *The Mod Squad* and *Mission: Impossible* and pretend that our living room couch was our getaway car. I'd tell Vern, "Jump out the window and roll across the floor!" and he'd do it.

We smashed all sorts of things around the apartment. We didn't have a designated playroom; the playroom was the house.

There was the living room, our room, Mom and Pop's room, and the kitchen. That was it. As a result of that unfortunate floor plan, a lot of lamps and various knickknacks got busted while we tore around the house like tornadoes.

As Vern grew older, he was like the precursor to MacGyver. He was a crackerjack at figuring things out and always learned everything by doing it first, usually at my urging. If we wanted to teach Vern how to ride a bike, we just put him on a bike and pushed him down a steep hill. He'd fall a few times, but before long, he would be pedaling like a pro.

Later, when we lived on Long Island, we "taught" Vern to swim at Roosevelt Pool by taking him to the top of the sixteen-foot-high diving board and forcing him to jump like it was a pirate's gangplank. The first time he hit the water, we had to pull him out of the pool. But the next day, in true MacGyver fashion, he dove in by himself and started swimming.

The whole time we were growing up in Brooklyn, even though he was just a kid, Eddie was intensely focused on what he wanted to one day become—a star. He had an insatiable appetite for television (he had the *TV Guide* memorized and never missed his favorite programs). He did impressions in front of the mirror, creating new characters and then, whenever the opportunity presented itself, performing them for the grown-ups.

It was like he knew he was destined for a specific kind of life and he was determined to make it happen no matter how much hard work it required.

But if you'd asked me at the time if I had a plan for how my life might turn out, the answer would have been no. I lived my life in the present, and circumstances depended on how the events unfolded from whatever I was focused on at the time. It was like, *All right, I'm supposed to be getting out of high school this year, but I'm not graduating because I've been cutting class— looks like I'm going to summer school. Or, okay, I'm out of school now and don't want to have to go to college, but everybody wants me to go, so I'll attend Adelphi Business School for two weeks until I'm kicked out for refusing to conform to the dress code. Okay, now I'm being kicked out of the house, looks like I need to go find an apartment and get a job. Then, I'm not making very much money at my job, I guess I'll become a thief.* I didn't have any plans; I just followed the wind and kept stumbling from one situation to the next.

In Eddie, I always saw the same drive that all successful people have: He knew what he wanted to do at a very young age. Most people in this world have no idea what they want to do with their lives. That's the category I fell into.

I'm not just talking about kids who say they want to be this or that when they grow up; I'm talking about an inner fire, a passion. Nobody ever told him he had to go practice his characters in front of the mirror, or that he better go do some improv study. Nobody said, "Yo, you better listen to the albums of these comedians if you want to be funny some day." Nobody ever told him that, because nobody ever had to. He did it on his own. But also, inside, he knew. From the time he could barely speak, Eddie used to go around telling everyone he was going to be famous. In fact, his first joke was when he told his family that he was going to be a superstar.

We all laughed and laughed.

The joke was on us.

While Eddie was focused on his dreams, I was more like Dennis the Menace—constantly getting into trouble. I tried a lot of things just because someone warned me I shouldn't.

Therefore, it was a great shock to everyone in 1968 when it was me who premiered in a major motion picture, Hal Ashby's *The Landlord.*

What happened was, The Boys' Club in Brooklyn put out the word that Hollywood was casting for extras in a movie that was shooting in the neighborhood. The casting slots were set up like a lottery; Mom entered my name and I won.

I appeared in a scene with Beau Bridges. Beau exits a building, sees kids stealing hubcaps, and yells, "Hey! What are you doing?!"

Then we run away.

That was the whole scene. But it was cool because I saw Louis Gossett, Jr., Pearl Bailey, and all of the other stars on the set. The whole experience of being on a movie set at nine years old felt very alien to me.

We had one movie theater in the Bushwick section of

Brooklyn—the Loew's Gates Theater, located around the corner from our place on Linden Street. That's where my friends and I would go to watch all the Clint Eastwood spaghetti westerns. I remember getting all dressed up with my family for the premiere of *The Landlord*, like it was Easter Sunday or the Academy Awards, and walking down to the theater. The running time of the film was 144 minutes, and I appeared on screen for maybe twenty seconds, but I could feel the excitement bubble over in the room when my scene came on.

Somebody yelled, "There he is!"

An odd epilogue to that whole experience occurred years later when I was with Eddie at Quincy Jones's house. Quincy had a glass case where he displayed personal items of Hal Ashby's—a wallet, some sunglasses. Also inside the case were Ashby's personal copies of scripts from films he had directed, including his script for *The Landlord*. It was the actual, physical script that was on set while I was shooting my first movie.

We shot *The Landlord* on Quincy Street in Brooklyn. I thought it was a wild coincidence that, twenty-five years later, the same script showed up in Quincy's house. Even the train that ran past our house and the Loew's Gates Theater in 1970 was called the Q-J train—*Quincy Jones*.

• • •

Despite my boyish mischievousness, my scuffles in the playgrounds and on the street, and my miraculous appearance in a Hollywood movie at the age of nine, first grade was when I got my first inkling that I might have the talent to be more than just a troublemaker my whole life. I wrote an essay titled "What Brotherhood Means to Me" that won a writing contest held for the entire first grade. That was the only trophy—or, for that matter, the only positive recognition—I would receive during my entire tenure as a student. I never received any awards for sports or academics, and most definitely not for good citizenship. But I remember how good it felt to be recognized and singled out by my teachers and peers for using my mind instead of my fists. I had no way of knowing then that, years later, I would return to my love of writing to pen screenplays for major motion pictures. Some would never get made, but some would gross tens—even hundreds—of millions of dollars.

But the thrill of being recognized for my writing was short-lived. I was suspended for fighting in each of my first three years of school—once for hitting a teacher. In those days, corporal punishment was acceptable. Teachers might have you stick out your hand so they could bang it with a ruler, or they might come up with more creative ways to keep you in line. One time, in the second grade, I had had enough, so I hit the teacher back. That got me suspended.

The principal said, "Don't come back to school until you bring your parents in with you."

That meant I had to go home and tell Mom and Pop that they needed to take a day off work to straighten things out at my school. That wasn't a conversation I was looking forward to having.

Public school in Brooklyn wasn't so bad, but things got much worse when the school system started busing us out to Queens in the late 1960s. I had just returned from a summer upstate, courtesy of The Fresh Air Fund, where I was exposed to middle-class America in the form of separate bedrooms for each kid, yards, trees, lakes, boat races, and cookouts. Because I was hosted by a laid-back hippie family, I was also exposed to my first taste of wine, my first puff of weed, and my first view of white people doing the nasty (the cabin had no doors on the rooms). I was also, for the first time in my life, exposed to white people on a grand scale. I was encouraged by how welcoming and friendly they all were to me.

Then I went home and rode the school bus to Queens.

When we first pulled up to the school, white parents were lining the curb, waiting for us kids from Brooklyn. As we walked off the school bus, they screamed, "Hey, nigger, go home!"

Through television, I was vaguely aware of the Civil Rights Movement and what was happening, I assumed, predominantly in the Deep South. But this wasn't Selma, Alabama—this was Middle Village, Queens.

I had to walk a ways to catch the bus to Queens. Because of Mom's and Pop's work schedules, I knew that if I missed that bus, I could stay home for the day. Of course, once I got hip to that I tried to abuse it. I'd run back into the apartment with a big smile on my face and announce, "Missed the bus again!"

"Oh, really?" said Mom.

"Yep."

"You just missed it yesterday."

"Missed it again."

"Well, I'll let you in on a secret: If you know what's good for you, you won't miss it tomorrow."

The next time I missed the bus, I walked to school.

For a little kid, the walk to school was like a four-mile odyssey through all sorts of exotic neighborhoods. Along the way we passed a pretzel factory where the workers would give us a giant, steaming-hot bag of freshly baked pretzels. To this day I'm spoiled on pretzels. I'll walk around midtown Manhattan, see those vendors on the street, and just turn up my nose at their stale pretzels. My pretzel standards are very high.

Another stop along our epic walk to Queens was at a local fruit stand. As we passed by, the grocer would hand each of us a fresh apple or a peach to sustain us on our journey. It got to the point where we looked forward to the days we missed the bus. Not to mention we would arrive at school late, so the next thing we knew, it was lunchtime. The second half of the day would fly by and we'd be on one way back home to Linden Street.

Sometimes when we walked, I would see dudes riding the

back bumper of the school bus down the street. I decided to try it myself one day when I was about eight years old. I watched this guy ride the back of the bus all the way up to the stop, and then step right off just like he was walking. I thought it looked simple, so I stepped up on the back bumper when the bus stopped at the red light on Bushwick Avenue. I was planning to ride it across the street and step off at the next stop, just like that other dude had done.

Problem was, when it looked like the bus driver was slowing down to pull over and stop, he suddenly lurched back into gear and started driving again. At that point I had already committed to stepping off, so I went flying off the back bumper, my face and chest skidding along the pavement.

When I got home, Mom said, "What happened to you?"

"Nothing. I was playing football."

She would not have been pleased to learn I had fallen off the back of a moving bus.

On those occasions when I would invariably return home from P.S. 87 in Queens, dragging my tail between my legs, to tell Mom I had been suspended again, she would say, "Charlie, let me get this straight: Are you telling me that I have to take another day off work, and that we're now going to have less money as a family because you chose to act out?"

Losing a day of work was a big deal because Mom and Pop were working hard, saving all their money to buy our first house and move us out of Brooklyn.

After a game in 1974—the only one we won that year.

CHAPTER FOUR

ROOSEVELT

In 1973, when I was fourteen and in the seventh grade, my family moved into a house in Roosevelt, Long Island. We had our own yard and our own trees, and in our new driveway, Pop rolled up in our first-ever family car. It was the first house and car Pop had ever owned. He was thirty-one years old.

My first impression of Roosevelt was similar to the vibe I felt when I went upstate with The Fresh Air Fund: middle-class America, where kids had their own bedrooms, the parks had lakes in them, and people played strange games like tennis. I thought, *This is gonna be cool, man.*

But I soon discovered that what makes the 'hood is not what it looks like, but rather the people who live there. Roosevelt had a dark side. Mom and Pop were oblivious to the fact that we were living in such a bad neighborhood. They looked around at those freshly mowed lawns, those shady trees lining the sidewalks, and they couldn't imagine the element that was lurking in the shadows. But it was there, and it wasn't just passing through. Roosevelt looked like a picturesque, quintessential American suburb, but it was a rough place, filled with a lot of bad dudes—many of whom I would soon encounter.

I started attending Roosevelt High School. Roosevelt High may be the alma mater of Chuck D and Dr. J, but it was also featured on a national television show that named it the worst school on the East Coast. Roosevelt High's reputation was so bad in the 1970s that when Vernon applied to colleges, one of the registrars told him he'd need seven years to get his bachelor's degree—three more than normal—because he was a Roosevelt graduate.

Roosevelt High was the kind of school where the freshman class's top bully could roam the halls flicking a switchblade and nobody would stop him (perhaps someone should have, since he went to prison later that year for murder). It was the kind of school where a teacher could impregnate one of his students and not be charged with a crime. Years later, that same teacher approached us, with his family, in a club in Los Angeles.

He said, "Eddie, do you remember me?"

Eddie said, "Sure I do. You're a pedophile."

The look on that dude's face was priceless.

· · ·

Before long, wandering the corridors of Roosevelt High, I became enamored with a rather large girl who possessed the biggest ass in the school, and I was fascinated by it, drawn to it like a moon orbiting a massive, radiant planet. Besides her ample bedonk, I also liked that she carried herself like she was older than she really was. I liked acting grown-up myself, so she was right up my alley. We started seeing each other, and everything was going fine until I started mentioning her name around the house. The problem was, her name sounded like a name a dairy farmer would give one of his best milk producers.

My family would tease, "Her name is what? That's a cow's name, man. Does she wear a bell?"

"No."

"Does she eat in the cafeteria or go out and graze on the football field?"

I suffered a barrage of Eddie's best barnyard humor. Obviously, he was a talented comedian, so he easily got my parents and Vern laughing pretty hard about it, too. He had also picked up some sharp bathroom humor from those Red Foxx and Richard Pryor albums we used to overhear while the adults huddled around the record player back in Brooklyn. Eddie had everyone laughing about my new girl.

Everyone but me.

One afternoon my girl came over for her first visit. I told everybody the jokes had to stop. She arrived, but before my family could meet her, she asked to use the bathroom. I showed her to the one downstairs in the finished basement, where she proceeded to take the biggest dump of her young life. A horrendous odor consumed the entire basement and started seeping up through the floorboards. Eddie came around to find me, sniffing his nose in the air.

"Goddamn, somebody's got the whole basement fucked up."

I said, "Why don't you go on back upstairs?"

"Who's in there?"

"Never mind who's in there. A friend of mine. Go back upstairs."

Eddie crouched down on the floor and peered under the door.

"Whoever it is, they're wearing green Pumas and gripping the sides of the porcelain like they're at the top of an amusement park ride."

"Yo! Why don't you go upstairs, man?!"

Eddie went upstairs. I heard him ask Mom who was downstairs fertilizing the basement. After that, all I could hear was Eddie's hysterical laughter.

In school, my academic efforts impressed no one. I began to master the art of earning 65 percent—the minimum passing grade—for every test I took and every class I bothered to attend. I was probably smart enough to earn much better grades, maybe even A's, but I chose to do the least amount of work required to get by. I was restless in Roosevelt, searching for something to focus my mind on. At the age of thirteen, Eddie was already performing for live audiences at clubs like The Dolphin's Cove, getting paid ten dollars to crack jokes for a roomful of grown-ups. He was dropping well-rehearsed Richard Pryor lines like, "My father died fucking. He was fifty-seven when he died. The woman was eighteen. My father came and went at the same time."

The first time I saw my brother perform in public was in a talent show at the Roosevelt Youth Center. He could already rattle off more than a hundred impressions of celebrities. I thought he was better than Rich Little, who, at the time, was the most famous impersonator in the world.

Eddie wore a white suit and sang Al Green's 1972 hit "Let's Stay Together." All the girls went absolutely crazy, like he was really Al Green. It hit me right then that my brother possessed an extraordinary talent. It was one thing to watch him practice his impressions around the house, but it was quite another to see him through the eyes of the people who would one day be his worldwide legion of fans and admirers.

I screamed at the top of my lungs, "That's my brother!"

I cried a little, too, out of sheer amazement. I still count that night as one of the proudest moments of my life.

My brother had a special gift for performance. Was I ever going to discover a similar gift in my life? I considered that question often, and when I did, my mind would simply go blank—as blank as when I first took the stage at the Laugh Factory years later and had absolutely no clue what I was going to say.

At Roosevelt High I would cut classes, do well on the tests I needed to pass, and earn the grades that would send me on to the next level. I have a photographic memory (which was very helpful later in life, when I started acting and memorizing scripts). I used to study for finals the night before exams and go in and pass them all, based almost entirely on my ability to memorize. I could learn in a day what took other students a week, a month, or a whole semester to absorb. Did I use this experience as an opportunity to see my potential, to realize that I had a brain in my head? No. I just enjoyed feeling like I was putting one over on the school and on Mom and Pop. Passing was passing as far as I was concerned; I had no ambition for higher achievement.

A photographic memory is a very powerful tool in the hands of a motivated individual, but I never considered the things I was doing back in high school to be any measure of my intelligence. I always chose the path of least resistance. No one at Roosevelt High recognized or nurtured any glimmer of potential in me, or encouraged me, or rode my ass to strive for anything. They all just let me slide by. Everyone, that is, except my parents. If not for them, I would have been completely adrift in my life.

Unlike Eddie, who was confident in his innate potential early on, I had energy without focus. It seemed the school didn't know what to do with kids who had fertile minds but could be difficult to handle. You were either a good kid or you were trouble. You weren't allowed to be both.

Today, my kids go to after-school tutoring sessions even though they're getting passing grades in all their classes. When I was at Roosevelt, tutoring was considered special instruction for kids who couldn't make the grade. Tutoring used to be designed to help kids limp to graduation; now it's an extra edge that helps them achieve at the highest levels. And after tutoring, kids are usually off to karate class, soccer practice, archery, ballet, Chinese-language class, parasailing, or whatever else, and then it's home for dinner, homework, and bed. We didn't have schedules like that.

I would get home from school at three o'clock and do my homework, and then the rest of the day was mine to find whatever trouble I could before dinner.

That's when I started to head over to Centennial Park.

In Roosevelt, there were two parks: Roosevelt Park and Centennial Park. The law-abiding, upstanding citizens of Long Island tended to frequent Roosevelt Park, while Centennial Park played host to all the pirates and buccaneers. Naturally, that's where I began to spend the majority of my free time.

When you start hanging with a group of people every day, their lifestyle slowly becomes your lifestyle. The lifestyles of my new group of friends in Centennial Park were those of thieves and addicts.

When I was about fifteen, the predominant drug on the

street was heroin. People were injecting it into their veins to get their fix. I never did heroin—not because I felt I was better than anybody, but because I was afraid of needles. Turns out, that fear of needles is one of the many factors in my life that contributed to saving it.

So instead of hard drugs, I started to experiment with weed. My first hit of the sticky icky with my hippie Fresh Air Fund hosts when I was nine years old was weird enough. But then, in an irony of all ironies, my earliest personal stash of weed came not from a dealer in Centennial Park, but from Pop himself— even though he didn't know it.

On one of my typical afternoons of searching through every closet, cabinet, and drawer in the house while my parents were at work, I discovered a fat bag of weed hidden in Pop's top dresser drawer. Apparently what happened was one night Pop went to a neighborhood party, and while he was there, he got pretty giddy or whatever, and somebody handed him a bag of dope. Pop never smoked weed in his life, but he brought it home anyway, probably because it was a gift. That bag sat in his drawer for at least four years. Over the course of that time, I would sneak into Pop's drawer and roll a joint, a little pinch at a time. Then one day Pop looked in his drawer and mumbled to himself, "Wait a minute. This was a full bag of weed. I never smoked any of it. And now it's gone."

He started yelling, "Who smoked this goddamn weed? I know who! Charlie smoked it!"

Damn. Caught. There was no way out of that one.

In 1974, when I was fifteen, a friend from Centennial Park asked me if I'd ever tried acid.

He said, "You trip on it, man. It makes you laugh. Hysterically."

So we got some tabs of blotta acid, little white squares with blue dots on them. I don't know what's in that shit—all I know is it made us bust out laughing right in people's faces.

One day, a group of five of us each did a hit, piled onto a train on the Long Island Rail Road, and rode it up to Penn Station. We spent the entire ride laughing uncontrollably. There was a dude sitting near us who looked just like the old-time, big-nosed singer Jimmy Durante. He had one of those noses where you could see every blue vein pulsing through the surface of the skin. We all stared at his nose, transfixed. One of us noticed that his nose resembled a subway map and started pointing out the various stations along the route, and other points of interest.

"Next stop, Canarsie!" one of us would call out, pointing at the map on the old man's nose as we howled with laughter. "Stand clear of the doors!"

Even though the old dude was a dead ringer for Jimmy Durante, one of my friends starting doing an impression of W. C. Fields: "Yes, my little chickadee."

This caused the whole group of us to double over, convulsing with hysterical laughter. All the other people on the train looked at us, wondering what the hell we were laughing at. Finally, one of my friends figured out that we had it all wrong. Suddenly, he barked out, "Yes, we have no bananas . . ."

The moment he said that, the entire train knew exactly who we were all laughing at, and why, and then they all started laughing, too. There we were, a dozen or so of us in a train on the L.I.R.R. (some of us tripping on acid, most not), busting out laughing at this old dude's ruddy, dimpled nose.

For his part, the gentleman whose schnoz was the center of all the unwanted attention did not find the situation as amusing as the rest of us did. On the contrary, he was quite angry. Then, while I was staring right at it, one of the blue veins in the old man's nose ruptured. It exploded right before my eyes, spraying a fine mist of red blood all over the car like a busted fire hydrant on Linden Street. The old man furiously stormed off the train at the next stop.

To this very day, I don't know if that really happened or if it was the acid.

When I turned sixteen and was a freshman at Roosevelt High, I was in full swing in Centennial Park. Finding trouble was the order of the day, every day. I hooked up with a dude I'll call "Terrence" and decided to take him shoplifting with me. I told him exactly what to do and how to do it, but Terrence chose to ignore everything I said and, subsequently, got nabbed.

A month later, Terrence and I were back hanging out in the park. We had reconnected and everything was cool—or so I thought. We started messing around, play-wrestling with each other, and Terrence got me turned around into a headlock. Once he was satisfied I couldn't escape from his grasp, he said, "Okay, Charlie, this is a real fight."

I realized he was trying to jump me, so I started twisting, swinging, and scrapping with him. A couple friends had to step up and pull us apart.

I said, "Just for that, Terrence, I'm gonna get you back."

Two weeks passed. During that time, I told everyone what I was going to do to Terrence once I got my hands on him. Then I described, in great detail, a series of very bad things. That was a stupid move on my part. Terrence soon got wind of my tough talk, and he prepared himself for the next time he ran into me.

One of my friends was dating Terrence's sister, so one night I found myself waiting in a car outside Terrence's house. I said, "All right, this is it. I'm gonna go whip his ass right now."

When I confronted Terrence he pulled out a pistol, pressed it against my forehead, and, with every intention of killing me to protect himself, pulled the trigger.

Click.

The round misfired.

Sometimes I think about that moment, about all the things that have transpired in my life between then and now, about my wife and children. I was fortunate to walk away from that situation. Most young men who work their way into that mess of trouble don't walk away; they don't get a second chance. Somebody was smiling on me that night. I was lucky.

But just because I was lucky didn't mean I was smart. My days of getting mixed up in trouble were just getting started. I had cheated death once, but I didn't learn my lesson.

My ongoing search to discover what it was that might ignite my inner fire left me wide open to make a connection with something meaningful and bigger than myself. That's how I became a member of the Five Percent Nation—more commonly known as the Five Percenters. I was baptized a Catholic, but the whole ritual of going to church, and that style of worship, never stuck for me.

It probably had a lot to do with the fact that my mother wasn't much of a churchgoer. Mom asked Eddie and me if we wanted to go to church but she never forced us to go. Eventually, she would send us off to church by ourselves on Sundays with money for the collection plate. There was a playground across the street, so we used the money to buy candy and play until we saw that services were over. Then we'd head back home.

Mom would say, "How was church?"

"Fine."

"What'd they talk about?"

"God."

She never took it further than that. Mom just wanted us to know that there was such a thing as God, and that we believed in God, we just didn't visit his house on a regular basis.

But when I was older, and the Five Percent Nation became popular with the crew I was hanging with, I was wide open to it. I was young and black, I'd been exposed to real racism by that point, and along came this alternative faith. It was something that offered an opportunity for me to feel good about myself. I was told that I was a black man descended from kings. That sounded good to me, and I decided I wanted to know more about it.

I'm not affiliated with them anymore—it was a chapter in my life that is now closed—but the Five Percenters believe that the Blackman is the original man, and therefore God. That the Earth is symbolic of the Blackwoman, and that through the inner esoteric powers of the Gods and Earth, people can transform and possess their true potential. It's a very pro-black religion, and the men who subscribe to its beliefs call each other God. Five Percenters believe the world can be divided into three groups: 85 percent who are blind to themselves and God and are easily led in the wrong direction; 10 percent who know the truth but teach lies; and the 5 percent who are the poor righteous teachers of wisdom, knowledge, and truth. It includes all kinds of systems, such as Supreme Mathematics.

When I first started getting fanatical about being a Five Percenter, I changed my name (unofficially) to Omar Allah, stopped eating pork, dressed differently, and started spouting off every night at the dinner table about Black Nationalism.

Mom said, "Hey, *Omar*, how are you going to master Supreme Mathematics when you can't even pass algebra at Roosevelt High School?"

Then she'd tell me to pass her the gravy for the delicious pork roast she'd just cooked and to keep my voice down while people were trying to eat.

Around the same time I became a Five Percenter, I also joined a street gang called the King Pythons. In Roosevelt in the 1970s—and in Centennial Park in particular—those two extracurriculars went together like pancakes and maple syrup. The leader of the gang was a dude who was practically old enough to be our father. Being a grown man, he was able to intimidate the members of the gang, most of whom were just boys. I watched him stab two of my friends for not bringing their dues to a meeting. The only reason we even had dues was to pay for his wine. He was a bad dude—he scared me, and I didn't scare easily.

We all had to make colors for our jackets so we could wear them to our gang meetings. A gang meeting consisted of us all assembling, then walking over to the next town to start fights. In the beginning, there was something about having those colors on my back that made me feel like I was part of something. That feeling of camaraderie made me willing to do things that I would never have done on my own. I enjoyed the sense of fellowship.

One afternoon I was inspired to run my first full-fledged

con/stickup job. There were no real guns involved or anything; it was just a game we ran on this dude who was flashing around a wad of cash.

I was sitting in the barbershop with four of my friends when some dude we didn't know walked in. He was about thirty years old, and something was definitely off about him—he was a little slow in the head.

He reached into his pocket, pulled out a wad of cash, and started counting it real loud: "ONE HUNDRED. TWO HUN-DRED. THREE HUNDRED . . ." All the way up to two thousand dollars. Each time, he slapped a crisp hundred-dollar bill down on the table.

The barbershop got real quiet. Then the dude announced he was headed over to Centennial Park, gathered up his money, and left. I turned to one of my friends and said, "Run down to Woolworths and buy one of them plastic cap pistols."

My plan was simple: We were going to follow him to the park and wait for him to go into the bathroom. I said to my friend, "When he goes into the bathroom, you follow him and go to take a piss. I'll come in and put the gun to your neck like I'm gonna rob you. You take out all your money and put it in the sink, then I'll turn to the dude with the two grand in his pocket and say, 'You, too.' He'll be looking at me with the gun on you, and if you act like you're horrified, he'll be horrified."

It was a good plan, and it worked—with only one hitch. As we were running the con, another guy walked into the bathroom and saw what was going on before we ran out with the cash.

Two days later I was back hanging in the park and the same guy who'd stumbled in on us pulled a knife on me and started talking about "our" money, asking me where his cut was.

I said, "What cut? All you did was walk in to take a piss."

He disagreed with my assessment, saying he felt his contribution should be recognized monetarily—his contribution being not thrusting his knife into my belly that very moment.

He said, "I'm gonna kill you."

Things didn't look good.

Then I noticed that the dude was wearing a T-shirt that read PEACE GOD. He was a fellow Five Percenter.

I said, "Hey, if I'm a black man and you're a black man, and you and I are supposed to be God, and the white man is the devil, why are you trying to kill me? You ain't white."

That shit fucked him up. He had to stop and think about that one, and he paused long enough to relax his grip on the knife and forget his original purpose for engaging me in conversation. Once again I had cheated death and been given another chance.

Because of episodes such as guns being pressed to my head and knives being poked in my belly, the seed of an inner conflict was beginning to take root in my mind and body. Somewhere inside Omar, the gangbanging Five Percenter, Charlie Murphy didn't like who he was becoming. But even though I was starting to analyze my decisions and scrutinize my actions, I wasn't yet ready to do anything to change my situation. I was still very much swept up in the pride and spirit of belonging to a unit, something bigger than me. I felt a sense, however misguided, of place and purpose.

Before long, I ascended in the gang to the rank of capo, a level that placed me in charge of my own division. My Five Per-center name was Omar, but my gang name was L'il Boss. Becoming a capo meant that I had done my share of fighting and started my share of trouble in Roosevelt and the surrounding towns. I was seventeen and I was barreling down the wrong track like an out-of-control locomotive. It was clear that things would not end well if I stayed on the path I was on.

But I didn't know how to change.

My little brother had direction—he was practicing his routines and performing in clubs at thirteen. The only direction I was headed was down, down, down.

And then I hit bottom.

One night a few friends and I were riding in a taxicab. One of my friends was carrying his father's pistol. On the spur of the moment, for what in our minds amounted to nothing more than a lark, we decided to rob the driver at gunpoint.

Running away from the cab, we thought we were so cool. But of course, we weren't. In fact, we were fucking idiots.

The next day we were all arrested. The next day! That was

my first time being in real trouble. Mom and Pop drove down and bailed me out. When we got home, they told me they didn't know if they were talking to Omar or Charlie, but both of us had to pack up our shit and move out of the house. I remember seeing the devastation on their faces. They were both so disappointed that I could act so recklessly, that I could be so ungrateful and careless with the life they worked so hard to provide for me.

I felt foolish.

I had no record of prior offenses (nothing I was caught doing, anyway), so I appeared in court and received probation. I had committed a felony. I was charged as a youthful offender on my first offense and handed three years' probation.

I had been presented with another opportunity to see the destructive path I was on. Of course, I ignored all the good advice and warning signs and, even worse, failed to keep my nose clean for those three probationary years. While I never committed any major crimes, in the third year I was arrested for petit larceny, loitering, and a few other misdemeanors. Taken all together, the crimes were a violation of my probation.

Mom said, "Charlie, you have to face the music. You have to go see your probation officer and get straightened out."

I didn't want to get straightened out. I knew straightened out meant they would review my probation violations and send me straight to jail. I avoided reporting to my probation officer for a while, but that couldn't last forever. When I finally went in to see him, he locked me up. I was sentenced to serve out the remainder of my probation in Nassau County Jail. I was going away for ten months.

Jail.

Wow.

The scariest part about jail was that it didn't scare me. On the contrary, I found many aspects of being locked up rather amusing. I suppose the scariest part of the whole experience was that I found myself living comfortably on the inside. I started to understand how guys could fall into an inescapable routine of cycling in and out of jail.

The food in jail was a lot better than I expected. (Remember, now, I'm talking about Nassau County Jail, not New York State prison—that's a whole other level of incarceration.) In jail, we ate meals like pancakes, scrambled eggs, and bacon for breakfast, and meat loaf and pasta for dinner. I never once recall complaining about the food. Chow time was also one of the highlights of the day because that's when all the fights would start and that would serve as our entertainment.

But the best part was that all my friends from Centennial Park were in jail with me. It was like being with my old crew, pretty much doing all the same things we would normally do while hanging out in the street: playing basketball, joking around, and fighting against one group or another over perceived slights.

The sad epilogue to my time in Centennial Park is that nearly everyone I knew there ended up dead from drugs or violence, or found themselves hanging out in a prison yard. Centennial in the 1970s was nothing more than a prelude to the cemetery or the joint. It was a gathering place for gamblers, pimps, thieves, drug dealers—you name it. We were the lost boys, and what we all had in common was that everybody hanging in Centennial Park seemed to be missing something in his life. I didn't have many friends, and my brothers were younger than me, so, thrust into a whole new environment after leaving Brooklyn, I was looking to connect with other people my age.

I seemed to fall into a group of people who were in similar circumstances. Unfortunately, as far as the laws of the land were concerned, I fell into the wrong group. I remember thinking at the time how cool those dudes were, living the lives of adults. I had to be home at night for dinner with my family, while those guys got to stay out as late as they wanted, doing whatever they felt like doing: shooting drugs, robbing, and getting girls pregnant. I was impressed by that. I thought they were living the good life. Looking back now, it's easy to see how naïve I was as a kid, but at the time those were the dudes I wanted to emulate.

In jail, I didn't feel scared. I could take care of myself. Pop had taught me how to box, and hanging in Centennial Park had taught me how to fight in the streets. I was always ready and willing to go, so I didn't have any problems in that regard. And anyway, I was always the guy trying to make everyone laugh, telling jokes or making up poems about the other inmates. Come to think of it, the county lockup was my first real crack at stand-up comedy.

Talk about a tough crowd.

I had a fellow inmate who, back in the neighborhood in Roosevelt, was one of the most feared dudes on the street. Once we got to know each other in jail, he confided in me that he couldn't read or write. Here was this big, tough thug who wouldn't let anybody else but me know he was illiterate, because he wanted me to sit with him while he dictated letters home to his mother.

And those letters were hilarious. He once dictated to me: "Dear Momma, this is your son. I need you to put thirty dollars in my commissary or a dude named Crunch will shank me."

"Stop right there, my man," I said. "You can't write that. Does your mother even know what a shank is? A dude named Crunch? She ain't even gonna understand this, bro. You need to say, 'Momma, a man with a knife is threatening my life. It is urgent that I give him thirty dollars . . .' "

My job in jail was in the kitchen. I learned that if I wrapped them up, I could fit about eight hamburgers in my drawers and then sell them when I got upstairs to my cell block. It always fascinated and delighted me that dudes would eat burgers that had been nestled beneath my nuts—and pay me for the pleasure.

My ten-month sentence ended on a Monday. Upon my release, Mom picked me up and drove me straight to the military recruiting stations; she was not going to allow me to reintegrate back into the neighborhood. I reluctantly agreed. It was a decision, and a moment, that would once again save my life.

Our first stop was at the Army recruiting office. Mom said to the recruiter, "I don't care what you have him doing: scrubbing jeeps, cleaning toilets. Just please take him."

The recruiter said, "You got a high school diploma, son?"

"Yes."

"Mmm hmm. You got a jail record?"

"Yeah."

"You can't come in."

Next we went to the Air Force recruiter's office. They told me the exact same thing the Army did. From there we drove over to the Marines.

On the way, I started warming to the idea of all the excitement, travel, and big guns involved in military service. I said, "Shit, the Marines will take anybody."

The Marines said, "Nope."

At the Navy office, the recruiter asked, "Do you have a criminal record?"

Standing there in front of that naval recruiter, who was my last hope of joining the military before Mom drove me back to what would, no doubt, be my reentry into the Centennial Park lifestyle, I paused for a moment. Maybe I had a premonition, because it wasn't long before AIDS and crack cocaine would descend on Roosevelt like the Angel of Death and the neighborhood's male population would be nearly wiped out. Drugs, and the scourge of AIDS, would soon roll through my old haunts in a wave of death and heartache, and I was on the precipice of living out one of two very different lives.

My running buddies in Roosevelt and I had a choice to make: We could die, we could go to prison, or we could get the fuck out.

I straightened up and asked the recruiter if he could repeat the question.

He said, "Do you have a criminal record?"

I looked him in the eye and said, "No."

A month later I tossed Omar Allah and L'il Boss on my smoldering ash heap of bad decisions and took the L.I.R.R. north to Fort Hamilton, Brooklyn, to be sworn in to the United States Navy alongside 125 other new recruits. It was 1978. I was eighteen years old and about to start my life.

The week before I left for boot camp, I watched the commercial for the Navy on TV. The advertisement made the prospect of a military life look incredibly fun and interesting. They even used the word *adventure.*

I thought, *Wow, this might turn out all right after all.*

Vernon and me—home on leave from the Navy, 1978.

CHAPTER FIVE

IN THE NAVY

From Fort Hamilton, Brooklyn, we flew on a regular commercial flight out of JFK Airport to boot camp in Great Lakes, Illinois. It was my first time on an airplane.

We arrived in the dead of night, piled onto a bus, and were driven to the Great Lakes Naval Training Center. All I remember about that bus ride is being really excited to be joining the military—right up to the point when the bus stopped, the doors opened, and the drill instructors ran on like raving maniacs. They screamed at anybody and everybody, four inches from our faces. They had no regard for our zones of personal space.

The D.I.s called us maggots, worms, pansies, candy-asses— names you hear only in the military. This began at one o'clock in the morning, after we'd already been traveling all day with only one government-issued box lunch apiece. While I sat there, a man screaming inches from my face, I started to have serious doubts about what sort of adventure the Navy was actually going to be. Of course, at that point it was too late. And I knew that as bad as it was, it was still better than whatever I would have been doing at that exact moment in Centennial Park.

Besides, I had already sworn my oath to the president and to the armed services of the United States of America. Not only was I still subject to civilian law, I was now also under direct authority of the Universal Code of Military Justice (UCMJ). That meant I had a whole new set of rules to familiarize myself with after I absorbed the initial shock of transitioning into my new military lifestyle. The military drills the UCMJ into your skull right from the start. For example, if you have any thoughts of desertion, they make you aware that desertion is a violation punishable by death.

It's unlikely anyone would be executed these days for desertion, but logic and fairness are not part of the indoctrination process—a process designed to aggressively wrench you from your civilian life and hurl you screaming into your new life as a member of the armed services. Plus, those D.I.s can be quite convincing. So convincing, in fact, that I bought into their whole spiel. The Navy's hook was deep in my belly.

Boot camp is designed to create a new reality around each recruit so that the military world becomes his entire universe. Think about it—when you have a friend or family member actively serving in the military, you see them maybe once a year. That's because the system is designed to keep them living in a world within a world. Whatever branch they serve in, their military life is all-consuming. If a service member isn't married, the military will find a way to occupy his time, chop-fucking-chop. They'll make sure he's married to his job.

I did not enjoy boot camp, but I was proud that I made it through. Graduating boot camp was a big deal for me. I watched plenty of dudes from my platoon drop out or fail to make the grade. I think my platoon began with about a hundred men, and by the time graduation rolled around, half were gone.

Boot camp certainly opened my eyes to the fact that people are not always what they seem. That's a valuable lesson for an impressionable eighteen-year-old to learn during his first real time away from home (except for jail, of course): You don't know what a person is capable of until he's been tested physically, mentally, and emotionally. You need to witness a man's resolve before you categorize him. I watched dudes do some remarkable stuff—good and bad. I saw the full spectrum, from the ultramacho dudes to the most absurd forms of wimpery that can be conjured up.

The biggest wimp I saw in boot camp was a dude with a body like Adonis. He was built like a world-class bodybuilder and I watched him get carried off on a stretcher, crying out for his momma. A grown man, crying for his mommy in front of his whole platoon. That dude hadn't thrown himself on a grenade. He wasn't bleeding with a head wound. He just didn't have the inner fortitude and mental toughness to take what was dealt to him.

As he passed by, sniveling and shaking, I heard someone say, "Wow. Someone should put two behind your ear, my man. You're fucking worthless."

Boot camp was a weeding-out process. For the first time in my life, I felt good about something I had accomplished. The challenge gave me my first opportunity to focus my misguided energy and untapped intelligence—the kind of focus that, despite all my searching, I could never seem to dial into when I was growing up in Brooklyn or roaming the streets of Roosevelt.

I thought I was a tough guy, but I learned that being tough isn't about using your fists, it's about using your mind. That was a lesson I would explore even more deeply later, when I discovered martial arts.

Right away, the military did three things for me: It saved me from a lifestyle of drugs and violence that pointed me toward oblivion, it gave me a purpose, and it made me feel I was a part of something bigger than myself.

For me, it took focus and guts to succeed in boot camp. I looked forward to serving my country in the armed services and I was proud when I dressed for graduation.

I'd taken the first step—a big step—but it was far from the last. The Navy came with its own set of problems, as I was about to discover.

• • •

The guys who make it through boot camp are at their best. Everyone is forced to look and act the same: same haircut, same clothes, same can-do attitude. You have no individuality, so you never get to know what people were really like in their pre-military lives. This has the effect of making all the guys seem like stand-up dudes.

Right after graduation, a top-notch sailor, who, for the purposes of this story, I'll simply call "Bill," asked me if I felt like going home with him on leave to visit his family in Gary, Indiana. I felt like I'd made some good friends in boot camp, and Bill was one of them. He was number one in our class: smart, athletic, a leader, the whole package. He had really found an outstanding outlet for his skills in the Navy. I had eight weeks' worth of checks in my pocket and I was eager to see new places. I was glad to have the opportunity to go investigate someone else's hometown, so I agreed to go with him to Indiana.

Bill had just bought a Ford Mustang with his boot camp money. We got on the freeway and Bill pulled into the first grocery and liquor store we saw and bought one of those one-liter plastic bottles of 7Up and a fifth of Southern Comfort. He poured out three-quarters of the 7Up, refilled the bottle with the SoCo, slid a straw in it, and pulled back out onto the freeway.

I said, "Hey, Bill, why don't you wait till we get to where we're going? That's a lot of alcohol for freeway driving, man."

"Don't worry, Murphy. I'm fine."

We drove along and I kept watching him, but he seemed fine and was driving safely, so I let it go. The whole way he kept slurping on that straw, doing a job on that drink. Sure enough, by the time we reached Bill's parents' house in Gary, he was completely inebriated.

His mother opened the door. Her shoulders sank.

"Oh my God, Billy. I thought you were gonna clean up."

That's when I realized that this was the way Bill normally was. He was a fall-down drunk, and his mother had sent him off to the Navy to get clean and sober.

Bill started crying in the doorway. "Oh, Momma, I tried."

I thought, *What the fuck? This motherfucker's having a relapse? I'm in Gary-goddamn-Indiana with no way to get back to the barracks.* I was beginning to realize I didn't even know this dude.

His mother seemed to be reading the horror on my face. She said, "Don't worry, sailor, we'll get you back safe. Bill just needs to sleep this off for a while."

So I sat there in Bill's house while he slept off his bender in the next room. After a while, he woke up and said, "Fuck this. I'm outta here."

He was my only transportation, so I got in the car with him. Bill was determined to drive across town to crash his sister's birthday party, which was already in progress. We arrived, and the first thing Bill did was get in a fight with someone at the party. I looked around and began to notice that his sister and all her friends were Gary police officers. One of them pulled me aside and said, "Look, I don't know who you are, but you better get this fucker outta here."

They didn't even care that Bill was drunk. They wanted him away from their party so bad that they let him drive. I climbed back into the passenger seat and Bill fired up the engine, squealed around the corner, and drove right over a fire hydrant. Water exploded straight up into the air. It was like an acid flashback to Jimmy Durante's nose erupting all over the car on the Long Island Rail Road.

Bill kept right on driving. He was running low on fuel, so he pulled into a gas station. This was during the gas embargo in the late 1970s, so after the attendant filled the tank with twenty dollars' worth of gas, he reminded Bill that he owed twice the reading on the meter.

"What the fuck are you talking about?"

"Sir, look: The whole country knows this. There's a gas embargo. I have to double the amount on the meter."

"I don't know nothing about a gas embargo. I've been away at boot camp. And besides, you're full of shit. Here's twenty dollars."

"You owe me forty."

"I owe you dick," said Bill. "Fuck you."

As the Mustang peeled away from the gas station, I said, "Hey, man, that's theft of services. You've got to go back."

"Fuck you, too, Murphy. Say one more word and I'll throw you outta my car."

Red lights started flashing behind us. Bill got pulled over by the police. He waited for the cop to approach the driver's-side door and say, "License and registration," and then . . .

ZOOM!

Bill stood on the Mustang's accelerator, spinning his tires into the shoulder, and rocketed away from the police cruiser.

Now we were the subjects of a hot pursuit through country and suburban roads on a slow crime night in Gary, Indiana. The cops were chasing us at top speed, and they weren't messing around—they fired four rounds into the back of Bill's car.

Bill plowed the car off the side of the road into somebody's yard, jumped out, and screamed, "Fuck you, motherfuckers! I'm going home!"

Bill spun on his heels and tried to saunter off, like he was Steve McQueen or something, while through the windshield I watched half the Gary police force converge on him and slam his face into the hood of the Mustang. When they pulled him back and cuffed him, his face was mangled, bruised, and caked with blood.

They yanked me out of the car and I started talking fast: "I'm not drunk. Here's my ID. My name is Charles Murphy, I'm from Roosevelt, New York, and I'm in the Navy. I barely know this crazy motherfucker."

A cop said, "What're you doing with this asshole?"

"We're in the Navy together. This is our first weekend out of boot camp. I had no idea he was this type of dude."

The cop handed me back my ID and said, "Go on. Get the fuck outta here."

"Whaddya mean, get the fuck outta here? Where am I? Which way to a public phone?"

"I said start walking, sailor. Or, if you prefer, I can throw your ass in jail tonight, too."

"I'm walking. This is me, walking."

They all drove off and left me. After the excitement was over and the neighbors had shut off their lights and returned to bed, I wandered the dark, quiet streets of Gary at two o'clock in the morning with no clue where I was or how I might get back to Great Lakes, Illinois. I was wearing my Navy uniform, so I considered walking up to someone's door, ringing the bell, and asking to use their phone. But regardless of the uniform, I knew my mad niggerishness at that early hour would scare the shit out of some sleepy-eyed Hoosier.

So I wandered aimlessly. By an incredible stroke of luck, I bumped into Bill's sister, the cop, who happened to drive past. I explained to her what had happened and we drove together down to the precinct.

As soon as she walked in the door, the desk sergeant shook his head and said, "Trust me, he's not getting out tonight."

Bill's sister drove me to the train station and I rode back to the base in Great Lakes. That was the last I saw of Bill, crackerjack sailor and platoon leader. Great sailor or not, they discharged his ass for that night's drunken escapades.

I thought, *If this is just my first week out of boot camp, maybe the Navy is going to be an adventure after all.*

After you graduate from boot camp and take evaluation tests to determine your qualifications, the military hands you a book listing all the different Military Occupational Specialties (MOS) and tells you to choose a job.

I scored well on my evaluations, so I had many jobs to choose from. I scanned through my book and stopped immediately on the word *engineer*. I thought, *Wait a minute. I can be an engineer. I'm qualified to become a thermodynamic engineer? Hmm, what does a thermodynamic engineer on a naval ship do? Oh, I will be able to chemically test water. Wow. According to this, it'll be like I'm a scientist. Yo! Sign me up!*

As it turns out, a thermodynamic engineer, otherwise known as a boiler technician, works down in the brutally hot belly of the ship. To this day, I don't know why the term *technician* is applied to that particular occupation. Working in the boiler room is the most unforgiving, loneliest job on the ship. You smell like fuel all the time (Jet Propulsion No. 5, or JP-5), just like a gas station attendant—one who works all day, *inside* the gas tank. You have permanent grime underneath your fingernails, like a grease monkey—not that I have anything against grease monkeys; I just never once envisioned myself working in that kind of environment.

Being a boiler technician was nothing like my vision of being an engineer and everything like my vision of being a mechanic—which I had no interest in being. We worked with valves, welded, cleaned boiler tubes, and performed all the other maintenance required to keep a naval vessel in tip-top shape. It was interesting to be learning something new—skills I would never have chosen to master on my own—but I never looked at my MOS as a lifelong vocation. The civilian counterpart to my job would have been to work for something like an insurance company, inspecting boilers in buildings. I didn't have any desire to do that. The only reason I took the job in the first place was because I was seduced by the word *engineer*.

That wasn't the last time the Navy would disappoint me—far from it. I was about to learn that life aboard ship is hard, but being a black sailor in a white man's Navy can make your life a whole lot harder. Especially if, like me, you're the type of person who, when the bullshit starts kicking in, you kick back.

I was stationed aboard the USS *Joseph Hewes* FFT-1078, a fast frigate out of Charleston, South Carolina. The ship's mission was to seek out and monitor submarine activity wherever it was sent to patrol, for about thirty days at a clip. We'd find an enemy sub, mark its location, and head home. There was no war going on. That game on the high seas continues all day, every day, to this very day: us monitoring and noting the movements of the military assets of other nations.

Being stationed out of the Deep South meant we had a lot of dudes on ship with old-school Southern beliefs and mannerisms, which added a degree of tension to the execution of our duties. My feeling has always been that if you don't like me or don't want to interact with me in regular society because I'm black, you don't have to. Nobody's telling you to talk to me, live near me, or even stand around me. You don't have to have anything to do with me. In fact, as far as I'm concerned, you can design your whole goddamn life to avoid me, if that's what you want.

But if you bring that attitude into a military unit, it's like forcing two negative poles to connect. One aspect of being in the Navy that I'll never forget, or forgive, was the tolerance of a racist environment that existed practically unchecked. The attitude my superiors fostered was that racism was unfortunate, but it was simply the way things were. There was nothing I *could* do about it, and nothing they *would* do about it.

My first week on the boat, we were under way and I was posted at the first watch station with the burner man, whose job was to sit in front of four windows, watching a jet gun shoot fuel into the boilers. If he turned one of the guns on or off, it affected the heat, which generated or decreased steam and moderated the speed of the ship. The burner man was named Prescott and, as the ship went through its maneuvers, his job was dictated by bells ringing down from the control room.

Prescott was a real chatterbox. He was talking to me the whole time he was supposed to be paying attention to his duty. Suddenly the bridge radioed down to the fire room, "What the fuck are you guys doing down there?! We said go two burners in!"

I was new, so I didn't know what the fuck was going on. Then I looked up and I saw what appeared to be a caveman right out of the Museum of Natural History jumping down through the hatch. This beast came storming toward Prescott and me, all the while pulling his belt off through the loops. I thought, *What's this motherfucker think he's getting ready to do with that belt?*

When he reached where we were standing, he grabbed Prescott, bent him over, and started spanking him. He was giving a grown man a lashing with his belt! When he finished whooping Prescott, he scowled at me, threaded his belt back through his pants, and climbed up through the hatch.

I said, "Yo, man, what the fuck is goin' on around here?!"

Prescott said, "Aw, I deserved it."

"Deserved it? You deserved a spanking? You dudes got some weird shit goin' on down in the boiler room."

I imagined the ghetto-style thumping my boys from the King Pythons would have administered to that caveman son of a bitch. I may have been a newbie in the Navy, but after Roosevelt High, Centennial Park, and Nassau County Jail, if that dude had tried to bend me over and spank me with his belt, we would've had to throw down. And as it turned out, that would not be my last run-in with the caveman.

There was always an undercurrent of racial disharmony pulsing through the ship. A few years into my enlistment, I saw one brother get into it with some hillbilly from West Virginia.

The hillbilly said, "Lookee here, nigger, you mind yerself when you talk to a white man."

Now, this wasn't 1945 in the segregated military—this was the early 1980s. And the black dude he was talking to wasn't from West Virginia. Where he came from, people didn't talk to one another that way. So the brother had no choice but to stomp that hillbilly's ass. After the dust settled, they both got sent up to captain's mast, which is a shipboard discipline proceeding where punishment is handed down.

The captain said, "Why'd you hit him?"

"Because he called me a nigger."

"Well, are you a nigger?"

"No, sir, I'm not."

"Good. That's why I'm sentencing you to ninety days. You're not a nigger, so obviously you're a racist because he called you one and you reacted. If you're not a nigger, how can he make you angry by calling you one?"

Huh?

Does that make any fucking sense? I look at that exchange now and still can't figure out what the fuck that captain was saying. But even if I was able to untangle that knot, it made no difference anyway. There's no logic—let alone justice—in the message the captain was trying to convey. That's just a small glimpse into the Navy I was up against.

Meanwhile, I was sweating away down in the boiler room as an engineer with the only other black dude in the division, Michael. Before I arrived on the scene, it was just Michael working down there, all by himself. Because of that, there was a lot of open, flagrant racist activity going on that I just wasn't going to stand for. Michael was on his own for a long time, so his way of dealing with it was to just try to get along. But I have never been that type of dude. I bumped up against my own pop when he told me to do something, so some snaggle-toothed peckerwood didn't stand a chance if he was going to refer to me as a "nigra." Unfortunately for those crackers, my attitude of self-respect created an immediate conflict in the fire room.

I told them all straight up, "None of you are gonna be calling me 'nigger,' so get over that disappointment real fast and let's move on."

What those hillbilly dudes tried to do was use incendiary language and plain, old-fashioned ignorance to break down the level of another man's humanity. That was their whole game. But the funny part was, those dudes calling me—a middle-class guy from New York—a "nigra" didn't look like they could operate a public telephone before joining the Navy.

My whole philosophy was simple: I joined the Navy to serve my country, not to serve bigots. My constant resistance made them uncomfortable and, eventually, very angry. Everything was going lovely for them before I showed up. Then I had to come along and spoil their Navy.

As I continued to speak my mind, they would go off into their Klan corners and grumble about "that uppity nigger, Murphy, from New York." They decided they wanted to teach me a lesson, so one night, while I was on watch in the middle of a storm, the boat rocking in deep rolls from starboard to port, a call came over the radio: "Murphy, c'mon up here to the control room."

I got up there and said, "What?"

"We want you to take out the trash."

I was an E4 at the time, and with that rank I wasn't supposed to be hauling out any trash, but I wasn't looking to start trouble unless it was absolutely necessary. So I lugged the giant garbage bags topside, to the watertight door that led out to the deck. The door had a lever and a series of ellipticals for sealing it shut, protecting the hull from taking on seawater in a storm. I opened the door—which was heavy—and was getting ready to step out with the garbage just as the ship rolled downward in a swell.

If you watch any of those shows on TV like *The Deadliest*

Catch, with those crab fisherman in Alaska, you know that the deck can be breached by huge waves. The boat can take that kind of beating, but if a human being is on deck under a big enough wave, he's going to be washed overboard.

As I began to step through the watertight door, I heard a sound I'd never heard before and have never heard again since. It was like I was standing in the heart of a tornado. I looked out and saw the darkness suddenly illuminated by the small flicker of light cast from a sodium lamp behind me. The darkness wasn't the night sky—it was a wall of water surging toward me, taller than the door I was stepping through. I leapt back and slammed the door shut as a towering wave of seawater exploded against the other side.

BA-BOOM!

It felt like a city bus had collided full speed with the other side of that door. If I had been half a second farther out that door—if my leg had still been hanging over the lip—it would've been chopped off by the force of the water. Either that, or I would have been washed over the side, never to be heard from again.

I stood heaving against the door while, outside, the wave rolled back into the black, churning ocean. I started piecing together what had just happened. I thought, *That's exactly what those motherfuckers up in the control room wanted to happen.*

The only wrinkle was, I survived.

I said, "Fuck the garbage," and headed back downstairs.

A while later, they radioed down again and said, "Murphy? You take the trash out?"

"Nope."

Silence.

"Murphy, c'mon back up to the control room."

I climbed up there again and, before they could open their mouths, I said, "Look, man, I know what you're doing. I think you're all well aware of the weather conditions we got tonight. I'm not stupid, and I'm not gonna let you kill me. You want the trash taken out? You take it."

The guy I was talking to was the very same caveman who had jumped down through the hatch and given Prescott the burner man a spanking like he was his daddy.

"You know what, Murphy? What you don't realize is that, around here, no one tells me no. I don't care if I tell you to go scrape a barnacle off the bottom of the ship in the middle of a goddamn typhoon. When I give you a direct order, you follow it."

"Listen, man, I just can't respect what you're saying. You sound ridiculous."

"Really? Well, the next time I tell you to do something and you don't do it, I'm gonna slap the shit outta you, boy."

I felt the hot rush of adrenaline surging through my veins like I was back in Brooklyn or wilding through the streets of Roosevelt. This Neanderthal motherfucker had unwittingly invited me right into my element.

"Well," I said, "if that's your plan, then do yourself a favor:

Ball up your fists. Slappin' me ain't gonna do you no good. You don't slap a man. I'm just telling you, you'd better go for the knockout. Because that's what I'm gonna do to you once you lay a hand on me."

The room froze in stunned silence. Caveman was the alpha male in the hole, and no one had ever stood up to him. We stared each other down, but it never came to blows.

After that encounter, things got pretty rough for me. I've never had a problem doing my job or working hard, but I certainly didn't join the military to face off with racist punks like that dude. In my opinion, his personal views were irrelevant. We all had a job to do.

I learned a lot of lessons about human nature in the military. The bottom line is, there are pockets of stupidity and racism everywhere in this world, not just in the Navy. It's a shame, too, because we're all on the same team. Especially in military service, where there may come a day when I've got to save a dude's life or he has to save mine. In situations like that, race doesn't come into play.

I joined the Navy to escape a cycle of destructive choices, to accept discipline into my life, and to help me along in my search for my own inner fire and passion. I didn't sign up to be abused, demeaned, or made into a spectacle. That's why I never backed down from racist thugs, and that's also why I never participated in any of the shipboard hazing rituals supposedly concocted to make me a "real man."

One of those rituals was called shellbacking. Shellbacking is a naval custom for crossing the line, or sailing over the equator, and it's sold to you as your induction into an elite maritime fraternity. But to be officially recognized as a member of that fraternity—in essence, as a full member of the crew—you have to allow yourself to be brutally hazed and degraded by your shipmates.

They start with fire hoses made of canvas, they soak them in brine, which is concentrated sea salt, and roll them flat on deck to bake in the sun until the salt granules have hardened into glasslike shards embedded in the corrugated fabric. Then they take long, industrial-sized garbage bags they've set aside to fester for two weeks and lay those out on the deck.

Next, everybody participating in the shellbacking fiasco gets buck naked and crawls through the rotten garbage bags. On the other side, a gauntlet of dudes beats you with those jagged fire hoses. When it's over, and you're stinking and bleeding with your wrinkled joint hanging down, they shake your hand and call you "Shellback."

No thanks.

I was never going to let them do that shit to me. No fucking way.

They said, "Charlie, if you don't become a shellback then you're not really a member of the crew."

And I said, "I'm not really a member of the crew, anyway, re-member? I'm a nigra."

Another rite of passage on a Navy ship back then was called greasing. If you worked in an engineering space, part of your initiation into becoming a "true snipe," or a true member of the engineering personnel, was a hazing ceremony that consisted of guys holding you down, pulling off your pants, and taking a grease called bluing (used on valves when there's a nick in the metal) and spreading it all over your body. Bluing stains like a tattoo when it comes in contact with skin, and it takes a long while to wear off.

Then they take a grease gun filled with a thick utility grease (also very hard to wash off) and slather that all around your groin and ass-crack region. They finish off by dusting your whole body in ash and cigarette butts and leaving you tied up for a couple hours.

Needless to say, I've never been greased, either.

To recap: Shellbacking was meant to signify that I was a true member of the crew, and greasing was designed to prove I was a true member of the engineering corp. So, I guess, in those terms, I was never really a member of the U.S. Navy.

When fellow crew members confronted me about not participating in their homoerotic oceanic rituals, I said, "Lemme explain something to you fellas: I'm not a member of your club, and I'm not going to be. Who the fuck thought this shit up, anyway? As far as I'm concerned, there is no correct reason that involves you guys handling my balls. Okay? From my perspective, if a group of sweaty, cheering men have their hands all over my balls and up my asshole, they are not, in my humble opinion, doing anything pertaining to my oath to the president. So if one of you motherfuckers touches me, I'm killing you."

I had a lot of great times in the Navy, too. Despite the tough challenges I found myself facing, I liked performing my duty and was proud to serve my country. Racism was one of the ugly parts, but I also met a lot of stand-up, upwardly mobile, and disciplined people. The military gave me a gauge for how to seek out the right kinds of people to associate with outside a military environment. Away from the dark influences of Centennial Park, the military taught me the qualities to look for in a good person.

My first three years in the Navy were very difficult, but the second three were like being at camp. That was because I finally achieved rank. Once I became an E5, the caveman and hillbillies on the boat were severely limited in what they could do to me. Plus, I now knew my full rights under the UCMJ.

Months away at sea can make a man restless, if you know what I mean. We were all young guys and, outside of occasionally slathering each other's nutsacks with grease, there wasn't much of an outlet for all that testosterone and supercharged sexual energy.

One time, we had been out at sea for a few months without a port of call. Finally we sailed into Cannes, France, during the Cannes Film Festival. Little did I know at the time that my first visit to the Cannes Film Festival would be far from my last.

Cannes was bumpin'. We came pouring off that boat, months removed from any civilian contact, ready for some action. In short, we were all horny as hell.

Our one mission during liberty in France was to get laid. We were strolling around in our uniforms, trying to generate some interest from the local talent, when one sailor suggested we head over to the nude beach.

"Nude beach?!" I asked.

"Right over this ridge, on the other side, is a nude beach."

A nude beach was one of those things that had lived in the deep recesses of my pornographic imagination since boyhood, like some fantastical European myth—on par with talking unicorns and sober leprechauns.

"Yeah, man," said another sailor. "Everybody over that ridge is buck naked."

In my mind, that translated to "Everybody over that ridge, right this minute, is fucking."

My warped concept of a nude beach was that everybody must be there to have sex. I really believed that you could just walk up to whomever you found attractive and start fucking. I didn't know there was a protocol involved, as with any normal, fully clothed encounter between potential partners. When I was growing up, whenever I'd heard mention of a nudist colony or read about one in a magazine, I'd assumed the whole town was constantly naked and getting it on.

We were all so painfully horny, all we needed to hear were the words *nude beach*. Eight other sailors and I immediately stripped naked and crested the hill to look down on the nude section of the beach. We crouched on the rocks and waited, staring down at all those glistening Europeans. Slowly, they started to notice us and, one by one, they packed up their things and left. Before long, the whole beach was empty.

We must've looked like a pack of starved wolves with rock hard dicks, crouched on the hill, ready to pounce. We scared the shit out of those Frenchies. To this day, that remains the only time I've been naked outdoors. I think it would be difficult for me to live in a nudist colony; I can't imagine becoming so comfortable with everyone's nudity that I would never be aroused. I don't even go into my own kitchen with my balls out. If I ever reached a point in my life where I was just strolling around flaccid all day with big titties all up in my face, I'd be gravely concerned that something was seriously wrong with me.

Anyway, it's nothing new to say that when sailors had liberty, in addition to looking for companionship, we also got drunk and did crazy shit. We were highly trained fighting machines in our twenties, set loose on the inhabitants of strange and exotic foreign lands—such as the Caribbean island of Puerto Rico.

There was a real macho dude on our boat—a real-life rodeo cowboy from North Dakota—who always wore a cowboy hat and had a faded circle worn into the denim of his back pocket from his ever-present tin of chewing tobacco.

One night a group of us rolled up to a bar in Puerto Rico just as it was closing. The people inside said they were sorry, but they were done for the night.

The cowboy thought he was John Wayne. He said, "I'm not going nowhere, goddamn it. Whaddya mean the bar's closed? Lookee here, ya gal-dang spics, fix me a drink."

I started slowly backing away as a group of angry faces closed in on him. We were in Puerto Rico, not Bismarck, North Dakota. When those Puerto Ricans finished thumping that tobacco-chomping John Wayne, he had to get a medical discharge from the Navy.

Another time, after a liberty in France, we returned to the ship to find a flamboyant-looking French gentleman waiting on the dock, furtively watching each sailor reboard the ship. He stopped me and asked, in a heavy accent, if I knew a certain person on the ship. I couldn't quite make out the name he was saying, so I had him repeat it several times, until it dawned on me he was telling me the name of my new supervisor, who had just transferred to our ship. This officer had come in with a head of steam and had started hassling me right away. I knew it was going to be a long haul with that dude.

I said to the Frenchman, "Are you talking about so-and-so?"

"*Oui, oui!*"

"Yeah, I know him."

The Frenchman handed me a duffel bag, along with a scented

note. In the duffel was this officer's underwear, which didn't necessarily mean anything—but then I read the note (I'm paraphrasing):

Mon Cher,
Making love to your ass last night and sucking your ba-
guette was magnifique. *I can barely wait for your return*
to my bed. Consider sending for me to be with you in the
south of Carolina. Et cetera, et cetera. Until we meet
again, my sweet, buttery pastry . . .

Au revoir,
Frenchie

I was positively delighted. In fact, I found this development in my contentious relationship with my asshole (no pun intended) new supervisor most intriguing.

The next day at quarters, the officer was doing roll call. When he arrived at "Murphy," I said, "Present. Excuse me, sir, a moment of your time. I have something here for you that I believe you will be most interested in."

I handed him the duffel bag and the note. His eyes bugged open.

After that, we never had any problems with each other. Whenever I asked him for something, the answer was always yes, before I even reached the end of my sentence. He had no idea if I'd kept a copy of that note, but he knew I'd read it, and despite the Navy's encouragement of its sailors smearing one another's genitals in thick grease and hog-tying one another to chairs, that officer wasn't comfortable letting anyone know he had a male companion overseas.

Speaking of sexual liaisons, I had a friend on the ship with a profound stutter who everyone called "Doc." Doc was a real cool dude who was always quick to fight. We were on a Mediterranean cruise (known as a "Med cruise") to Europe, and I had brought along my Iceberg Slim books. Iceberg Slim's birth name was Robert Beck, and he was a real-life pimp who became an author. His books were very popular in the 'hood, especially with teenagers. I'd read all my copies already so I gave them to Doc.

As the weeks passed, I started noticing some not-so-subtle changes in Doc's appearance and demeanor. He started walking and talking different, and he shaved his head bald. When we pulled into port, he went straight out and bought a new wardrobe of bright, fancy clothes and expensive shoes. Iceberg Slim had had a profound mentoring effect on Doc.

After we returned stateside, I was out at a party and ran into Doc. He was drunk, telling all the girls he was a high-class pimp.

He said, "Gather 'round, bitches. I'm Doc, and I'm the new thing on the block."

He was actually trying to recruit girls to turn tricks for him. But clearly Doc didn't know what the fuck he was doing. He had learned all his moves and dialogue from a paperback novel and was in way over his bald head.

At least I was enjoying myself; the spectacle was pure comedy.

Doc left the party with a girl. He was apparently headed to a hotel to sample the merchandise and see if she was up to the standard for his new stable of bitches. We all wished Doc good luck and waved good-bye.

The next morning Doc showed up in the barracks looking like he'd spent the night trapped in a cage with a bobcat. His silky new clothes were shredded and his face and body were gouged and bleeding. That was the end of Doc's pimping career.

Another night I was out drinking with Doc and another sailor in South Carolina. We decided to pull into a bar for one more drink before calling it a night. Isn't that always the first sign of trouble?

We were following a mud road leading to a backwoods local bar when our buddy's tire got stuck, wedged deep in a rut. We climbed out to have a look. That car wasn't going anywhere. Our buddy doubled back to a pay phone, encouraging Doc and me to walk the rest of the way to the bar, have a drink, and wait.

When we entered the bar, it was the complete reverse of that scene in *Animal House* when the music stops and everybody turns to see the white folks stepping into the club. This time it was our turn: two young black dudes stepping into some shit-kicker bar straight out of *Deliverance*.

We ordered a couple drinks. Slowly, everybody returned to their woodchuck pursuits and stopped paying us any mind.

After a couple drinks, we thought enough time had passed for our buddy to have settled his business with the car and come inside. But what had happened was that, when he called, the tow truck was very close by and arrived right away. On the phone, the tow-truck driver told our buddy that pulling his car out of the mud would cost him fifty dollars. Then, when the car was free, our buddy handed the driver a hundred dollars and waited for his change. But the driver just ignored him and packed up like he was leaving.

Our buddy said, "Yo, where's my change?"

"What change?"

"You said the tow would be fifty dollars."

"Now it's a hundred, boy."

"What'd you just call me?"

"You heard what I said, boy. Now the tow is a hundred."

"Motherfucker, you're gonna give me my fifty dollars."

The tow-truck driver walked up to him and said, "You better watch how you talk to folks around here."

Then he slapped him.

About halfway through the process of our buddy handing that tow-truck driver the beating of his lifetime, the other rednecks in the bar noticed through the window what was going on. Doc and I were still drinking, with no clue what was happening outside.

Some hillbilly dashed into the bar, pointed at us, and yelled, "Them's his homeboys. Git 'em!"

As soon as I heard that, I turned toward Doc and saw a beer

bottle exploding over his bald, wannabe pimp head. A full-blown barroom brawl erupted, with Doc and me at the center of it, fighting for our lives as we ran toward the door. Fists and feet were flying. We were like the Spartans slicing our way through the Persians in *300*. We made it outside just as the police pulled up. My first thought was, *Hallelujah, the cops are here!* Then one of them stepped from his car and the first words out of his mouth were to a dude I was fighting.

The cop said, "Momma says when you get home tonight . . ."

I didn't stick around to hear the rest of that sentence. This was the Deep South, and I was fighting a cop's brother. I took off running as fast as I could.

I suddenly found myself trudging through a Carolina swamp infested with black adders and cottonmouths, wearing only a pair of Yves Saint Laurent loafers on my feet. It was the black of night and I had no sense of direction. All I knew was I couldn't slow down and I couldn't turn back. Miraculously, when I emerged from the swamp, I was right up the street from my house. That's fear for you. I must've smelled my way home.

Getting into scrapes alongside my buddies over the years seems to be a theme in my life. My philosophy has always been if you're hanging with Charlie Murphy and get in a fight, Charlie Murphy gets in a fight.

Once, I was on the road, and one of the comedians who used to open my show got into a tussle with someone. I jumped in to help. The problem was, I found myself in the middle of the action, defending my fellow comedian, only to look up and see him standing safely in the crowd, cheering me on. Needless to say, that was the grand finale of our touring together.

When my hitch in the Navy was coming to a close, they offered me fifteen thousand dollars to reenlist, and I took it. As a result of my training, I became what is known as Surface Warfare qualified. If you look for that qualification on a naval uniform, above the nameplate you'll see a pair of dolphins— chrome for enlisted personnel, gold for officers. That means that if the ship was ever disabled, I could take over and do another person's job. That was an accomplishment I was very proud of.

I can't say I enjoyed the process of transitioning to military life—being dominated all the time by what amounted to another parent—but I do believe that it brought out the best in me through the various mental and physical challenges I faced. It had the effect I was hoping for when I signed up straight out of Nassau County Jail: It forced me to grow up.

I got my first car while I was in the Navy, along with opening my first bank account, marrying my first wife, and having my first child. Those, and many more positive developments, are the good things I drew from my time in the service.

• • •

When I reenlisted, I had a 4.0 rating as a sailor. That afforded me the option to transition into training as a warrant officer or an officer of the line. I seriously considered serving my full twenty years and then retiring from the Navy. I always had a fascination with uniforms and used to envision what I would look like as an officer.

One time, I was waiting alone in the office of my division officer and I noticed his hat was on the desk. I placed it on my head and turned toward the mirror to see what I would look like. Like a scene from some horror movie, when I gazed at my reflection, I saw that my division officer was standing right behind me.

"You like that hat, Murphy? And before you answer, keep in mind: I don't give a shit if you do or not. Take it off."

In 1979, I decided to accompany Eddie, who was eighteen, to a stand-up gig at a party at Hofstra University on Long Island. I would later learn through my own hard knocks on the road as a comic that a party is never a great setting for stand-up comedy. The number one enemy of a great stand-up comedy experience, for both the performer and the audience, is distraction.

Comedy and music definitely don't mix. If there's music playing, people talking, and lights shining, the comic onstage gets lost somewhere in the mix. But even though this Hofstra party had music, lights, and talking, Eddie still managed to make everybody laugh.

Everybody, that is, but two sarcastic jocks standing off to the side. They started heckling: "Fuck this shit, man. This guy's not funny."

It was unfortunate for those two that I happened to be home on leave that night. I took exception to people jeering at my brother, disrupting his show, and ruining everybody's good time, so I had no other choice but to stomp the shit out of both of them.

Eddie could easily have dealt with two drunk hecklers at one of his shows. By that time, he was a true pro. But for me, when it came to protecting my brother, old habits were hard to break. That incident would be my first official confrontation working security for Eddie, a task I would perform through-out the next decade, during Eddie's meteoric rise into super-celebrity status and through all the odd and fascinating culture surrounding that lifestyle.

The next year I turned twenty. My naval vessel had been on a Med cruise for four months. As soon as the ship moored to the pier I ran to the nearest public phone and called home.

Mom answered and said, "Eddie's got some good news for you."

Eddie got on the phone and said, "Yeah, I just auditioned for *Saturday Night Live*, man. I'm up against Charlie Barnett."

I had heard of Charlie Barnett—he was famous. He had made a name for himself in the late 1970s, performing over-the-top live shows outdoors in Washington Square Park in New York City. I said, "You're up against him? That's rough, man. Well, at least you tried."

As the story goes, *Saturday Night Live* producer Jean Doumanian was going to hire Charlie for the show, but after a last-minute audition by Eddie, he gave the spot in the cast to him instead. Later, Charlie would earn minor fame as Noogie Lamont on *Miami Vice*. He died of AIDS at forty-one in 1996, but he certainly left his mark on Washington Square Park. I believe that's where Dave Chappelle met him and cut his comedy teeth, with Charlie standing beside the fountain, encouraging his talented new protégé.

I remember the very first time I was able to sit down in front of a television and watch Eddie on an episode of *Saturday Night Live*. It was November 5, 1983, and the sketch was James Brown's Celebrity Hot Tub Party.

I was lying in my bunk laughing so hard that tears were pouring from my eyes. That sketch remains one of the most hilarious things I've ever seen. Whenever they air retrospectives and tribute shows for *SNL*, that performance is always included, and is regarded as one of the all-time best sketches ever produced. When I saw Eddie explode like that onto the television scene, I knew he was going to be one of the biggest stars in the world.

Eddie's run on *SNL* lasted from 1980 to 1984. All that time, because of my reenlistment, I remained in the Navy. In 1982,

Eddie made his feature film debut in *48 Hrs.*, which grossed more than seventy-five million dollars. In the same year, Eddie appeared three times on *The Tonight Show with Johnny Carson*. We would talk on the phone and he'd say, "Charlie, when are you coming home, man? I want you to come head up my security."

I'd answer, "What can I tell you, man? I can't just come home. I reupped. I'm committed to serve in the Navy until my time is up."

In 1983, Eddie starred alongside fellow *SNL* alum Dan Aykroyd and Jamie Lee Curtis in the John Landis comedy *Trading Places*. That movie has made more than ninety million dollars to date and, at the time, helped solidify Eddie's reputation as one of Hollywood's most bankable rising stars. In August of that same year, Eddie recorded *Delirious*, stalking the stage in his iconic red leather suit, the jacket zipped open below his belly button. Somebody spent the time to figure out that Eddie used the words *fuck* and *shit*, combined, more than four hundred times in that performance. However many times he used them, what mattered was that Eddie had connected with the audience that night, and that performance lit the comedy universe on fire.

During another shore leave, Eddie put me in a *SNL* filmed piece called White Like Me. The infamous sketch features Eddie going through life as a white man, appropriately named Mr. White. (I'm sitting in a barber's chair in the sketch, getting my face covered in white pancake makeup.) Being there on the set for a bit that was going to run on national television and be viewed by millions of people was exciting and inspiring—and a world away from the boiler room on the USS *Joseph Hewes*.

My brother was living his dream, and I had a front-row seat.

While Eddie was blowing up on TV and in the process of becoming the biggest box office star in the world, I kept on working, committed to my reenlistment in the U.S. Navy.

In 1984, Eddie was invited to play a private show at the South Carolina home of the notorious racist and United States Senator Strom Thurmond, who was known mostly for his segregationist candidacy for president and for standing up in Congress to prevent the passing of the Civil Rights Act. Naturally, it was later discovered that Thurmond had sired a daughter by one of his black housemaids in 1925.

Thurmond wanted Eddie to come down to South Carolina, where I was stationed, and do a show in his house for his grandkids or something, like he was some fucking birthday clown. Eddie sent word back to Thurmond that he would do the show on one condition: Thurmond had to get his older brother an immediate, honorable, early discharge from the U.S. Navy.

Thurmond did it.

Then, as the date of the performance neared, Eddie was informed that Thurmond was sick, and Eddie never even had to do the show. Maybe ol' Strom was just too busy making more babies with his black servants, Thomas Jefferson–style.

Whatever the truth was, Thurmond honored his word to my brother and—*bip-bam-bop*—just like that, I was out of the Navy and headed home to New York.

Eddie and me at the *Norbit* premier in 2007. (Getty Images)

CHAPTER SIX

A FRONT-ROW SEAT

I was discharged from the military in 1984, and I arrived home when Eddie was in the final season of his five-year stretch as a cast member on *Saturday Night Live*. That year also saw the release of *Beverly Hills Cop*, featuring Eddie in his breakout role, Detective Axel Foley. That film (which grossed more than two hundred million dollars at the box office, beating out *Ghostbusters* as the biggest hit of the year) catapulted Eddie to international stardom. The movie, produced by Jerry Bruckheimer, won the People's Choice Award for Best Picture, was nominated for a Golden Globe, and made Eddie one of the most sought-after lead performers in Hollywood.

Which is just another way of saying that when I got home after six years in the Navy, everything was different.

For instance, we could roll up to any club we wanted and

just walk right inside, without paying a cent. After toiling away for so long as a thermodynamic engineer in the U.S Navy, that was a very foreign concept to me.

Inside the clubs, we had our choice of women. That's when Studio 54 was at its zenith. That place was so singular and unique, so specific to its time, it's almost impossible to describe. Nothing could mess with what was going on in that place. It's one thing to watch the documentaries and be aware of what was happening in Studio 54, but it's another thing entirely when you're living it. I feel fortunate that, at that moment in time, I was young and had incredible access to that whole scene.

You could be standing in Studio 54 talking to a girl for fifteen minutes before you realized she was buck naked and covered in body paint. Cocaine was piled high on the bar like little ski slopes. And, of course, people were having sex everywhere, constantly. That club was more like I imagined things would be at a nude beach than when I actually went to a nude beach.

I saw people from all segments of society in there, bumping and grinding. It was nothing like our society is today, with cell phone cameras and the whole run-and-tell mentality that's poisoned the culture. *Ooh, look what so-and-so is doing. Let's take a picture and sell it to a magazine. Let's post it on my blog.*

Now everybody's got an iPhone or a BlackBerry or a laptop and they're all hoping they'll see something sensational so they can upload it to YouTube for everyone to see. We're living in the era of the snitch. People ask, "Why aren't there any Studio 54s anymore?" Because Studio 54 could never exist today. We're all surrounded by a bunch of fucking babies who just want to tattle. *Look at her! Look what she's doing!* I always ask, "Why are you so shocked? It's not like a giraffe is doing it. That's a human being, doing shit that human beings do." *Oh my God, so-and-so is having sex with so-and-so.* Guess what? Your parents had sex, too. That's the only reason you exist on the other end of that Black-Berry, you voyeuristic little bitch.

Another adjustment for me was finding that Eddie was surrounded by all new guys in his crew. Everybody was looking good, they all had money, and they were all living the lifestyle. I had been living on a ship for six years; I owned two outfits. Nobody on a ship ever looks at you, laughs, and says, "That's the same shirt you had on yesterday." As a result, I had fallen far out of the loop, style-wise. I didn't know what to wear. I was completely disconnected with the societal norms for what looked good on a twenty-five-year-old man in the 1980s. Eddie could see I was perplexed, so he told me I could wear any of his old stuff that I wanted to try on.

The problem with that was Eddie had become a famous person. When someone is a famous person, they can wear things that other people should not wear. I soon learned that people tend to keep you honest when you're wearing clothes you should not be wearing. They'll say things like, "Charlie, why you got that green glitter jacket on? Where you performing at tonight?"

I was going out every night in Eddie's hand-me-downs, looking like flashy boxing promoter Butch Lewis: no shirt, five gold chains, chemicals in my hair, and wearing a glittery green bus-boy jacket.

I was also giving myself a perm every week. You're only supposed to perm your hair about every four months, but I was doing it every Saturday, burning out my hair with no gloves and no neutralizer. I'll be the first to admit, it was a weird time, and I didn't yet have a handle on it. In retrospect, I don't know that I ever did.

In Hollywood, there were men at the clubs wearing makeup and spandex. These were not homosexuals. On the contrary, the dudes wearing eyeliner and pantyhose were the ones going home with all the chicks. Androgyny ruled the clubs. It was the era of the big-hair bands with their tight leather pants and ruby red lipstick. I was just trying to blend in with my busboy glitter jacket.

One night, while I was sporting my glitter jacket over no shirt, the whole crew rolled into a disco club. The crowd turned toward the door and some dude whispered, "Wow, that's Eddie Murphy."

Someone whispered back, "Who's that behind him?"

"That's his brother."

"I didn't know he had a brother. What's he do?"

The first dude looked me up and down for a second, then said, "I don't know. He must be a magician."

I caught a glimpse of myself in the mirror. The dude was right: I looked like I was going to pull a flock of white doves out of my sleeve.

I was going out in public with no fucking shirt on!

From that era, I definitely have memories of some fashion atrocities I still can't live down. I would browse clothes on the rack that most everyone else in the clothes-wearing universe would regard as complete garbage, and I'd say, "That's me. I'll wear that."

I did all right and got my share of the ladies but, years later, my fashion crimes from that period still felt so ridiculous and shameful that I went over to my mother's house and burned every photo of me from those days.

When my enlistment ended in the Navy, Eddie hired me on at a very generous salary to head up his security detail. My responsibilities didn't really require a lot of brainwork. The main goal was this: Don't let nobody fuck with Eddie.

In 1984, when I saw Eddie perform stand-up before a sold-out crowd of fifteen thousand in Buffalo, New York, for his "Pieces of My Mind" tour, it was a life-changing experience. He had come a long way from parroting Richard Pryor routines at The Dolphin's Cove for ten dollars a night and singing Al Green to screaming schoolgirls at the Roosevelt Youth Center.

I traveled the nation and around the globe with Eddie while he performed his stadium shows, attended movie premieres, and went on press junkets. Everywhere I went, people would offer me cocaine, chicks would offer me blow jobs (et cetera), and all sorts of weird new folks with funny names and funny clothes were always crowded backstage at every show.

Like Liberace, whom I met backstage at one of Eddie's performances. At one time, Liberace was the highest-paid entertainer in the world. When I met him, he was wearing a white mink coat that was longer than Princess Diana's wedding train. Walking behind him, carrying the train of his coat, were eight muscular dudes. All I could think was, *Thank God he ain't black. If a brother rolled like that, they'd crucify him. Eight dudes carrying his coat!*

Speaking of eight dudes, what made working Eddie's security fun was that it was a tight group of eight of us who all got along together and—for the most part—kept Eddie, and ourselves, out of serious trouble. It was like our crew had been unleashed on America and the world. The adjustment period from my military lifestyle to this new reality took a long time. I wasn't just returning to civilian life; I had been transported to another planet. I was thrown into the world of celebrity, and it was an enormous culture shock. I now had full access to excess.

I went from rising at 0600 hours on the grinder (that was the military term for the concrete area where we would do our morning calisthenics) to going to bed at six a.m. on a worldwide tour: London, Germany, France, Tokyo, the Caribbean—and the accommodations were always luxurious, the best of the best. In a very short period of time, I went from famine to feast.

We were constantly traveling between New York and Los Angeles, with the occasional stop in the Caribbean and Europe (for work and for relaxation), as well as frequent trips to world film festivals.

It was during this period of the mid-eighties, all the way through the nineties, that I got the opportunity to meet some of the most famous celebrities in the world. And because of my proximity to Eddie's fame, I got to meet them all on a personal, casual level. They were Eddie's peers in the entertainment industry, which meant I wasn't meeting them when they were performing or when a camera was on them. We were just sitting on the couches in their living rooms or chillin' in their backyards. They were all beautiful, gifted people, but they were normal people, in every respect but one: They had great talent and they used that talent to earn themselves incomes that afforded fabulous lifestyles.

One of the pop-culture phenomena in full stride around 1984 was Michael Jackson. He was so famous that L.A. was infested with a swarm of celebrity look-alikes. People were going so far as to have their hair curled and their faces altered, and their clothes were identical to the ones Michael wore to perform.

One day I was hanging in Eddie's house in L.A. when the doorbell rang. I opened the door and it was Michael Jackson.

I said, "Oh, shit! Michael Jackson! Hold on, lemme go get Eddie."

I took one step away and thought, *Wait a minute. If that's Michael Jackson, why is he by himself? Where's his limo? Where's his security?*

He was just a dude on Eddie's front step who looked like Michael Jackson.

I turned back and said, "Motherfucker, you ain't no goddamn Michael Jackson."

Then I slammed the door in his face.

There were so many celebrity impersonators strolling the streets of Hollywood that Chippendales decided to host a Celebrity Look-alike Night. Eddie thought it would be funny to attend, so we gathered up the crew and went.

The show featured an all-star lineup of look-alikes: Michael Jackson (of course), Prince, Diana Ross, Mr. T . . . When I got there, somebody came up to me and said, "You're the best goddamn Eddie Murphy impersonator I've ever seen. You're gonna win this shit for sure."

During the show, the competition between the various look-alikes was fierce. I'll never forget how the two best Michael Jackson look-alikes faced off in a dance-off, just like in the movie *Zoolander*. The ill-fated dance-off soon erupted into a fistfight, with each impersonator furious over how the other was portraying Michael Jackson.

After they were cleared off the stage, and once all the scattered rhinestones were swept up, Prince took the stage. Well, sort of. This brother looked exactly like Prince, from the hair to the clothes, with all the little lacy frills, and even the platform boots. Except for one difference: He had a wide, flat nose spread across his face like KRS-One—who must be the biggest-nose-having motherfucker in show business. Take that nose and imagine it on Prince's face. I can't emphasize it enough: His nose was tremendous.

The lights dimmed and he started singing "Little Red Corvette." He had all the girls in the club dancing and screaming. Then he got to the part in the show when Prince would usually turn around and fall backward into the audience. Everybody would catch Prince and lift him back onto the stage.

Because he was Prince.

But this little dude with the pancake nose wasn't Prince. He was a Prince *look-alike*.

So when he fell backward into the audience, everybody moved out of the way. He fell about five feet off the stage—*CRACK!*—right onto his head. He was knocked out cold.

Then everybody scooped up his unconscious body and tossed him back up onstage like Raggedy Andy. It was one of the funniest things we had ever seen in our lives. Our whole crew just kept choking for breath, we were laughing so hard.

When fake Prince regained consciousness, he wobbled to his feet and stormed off the stage, clicking his little high-heeled boots, while the club howled with laughter. Maybe he hopped a plane back to fake Minnesota.

The grand finale was a dude who came out looking like Mr. T from *The A-Team*. He had the Mohawk, he was buff, and he had the same amount of gold looped around his neck as the real Mr. T—the only difference being that the fake Mr. T was covered in brass.

He sang a song that started, "I'm the type of guy that look like Mr. T. But they call me Mr. K, 'cause I'm . . . so . . . *klean*."

Whenever I think of that night, I always wonder what all those impersonators are doing today. They're all out there somewhere, walking the streets of some town with a face like Michael Jackson, or Prince with a giant goddamn nose.

Around 1985, I was on the set of a music video for the John Landis movie *Into the Night*, starring Eddie, Jeff Goldblum, Michelle Pfeiffer, and Dan Aykroyd. I was in the trailer with a bunch of people when my stomach started rumbling and churning. I knew I couldn't go to the bathroom in the trailer—not with what I had going on inside me. That simply was not an option.

I thought maybe I could squeeze out a silent fart and make myself feel a little better, but that wasn't a smart move with so many people around. There was no way of predicting what the damage might be. I decided to step outside and search out a new venue for taking care of my business.

As soon as I stepped out of the trailer, I was stopped by a crowd of people who wanted to stand around and chat. The rumblings in my lower intestine kept worsening, so I politely es-

caped that group and stumbled directly into another crowd. My lower-bowels situation was reaching a critically urgent stage; I was at DEFCON 2, and I started to panic.

Finally I spotted an area behind the trailer that was up against a fence. I knew if I could wedge back in there, nobody would be around to smell what I had cooking. I sneaked back and eased off a long fart. As soon as I finished I realized it was one of the ripest rips of my life. I thought, *I sure am glad I made a decision to hide back here, where no one can see me. I would be positively horrified if anyone were to discover that I, Charlie Murphy, am back here whippin' up this kind of nasty funk.*

The instant that thought crossed my mind, a beautiful woman stepped up to me with her hand outstretched and introduced herself: "Hi. I'm Michelle Pfeiffer."

Poor Michelle. Her eyes were red and watering. There was real horror in her face as she tried to make sense of what she was smelling. *Could it possibly be of this world?*

That's how I met the lovely Michelle Pfeiffer: in a cloud of my own mustard gas. She must've thought, *Y'know, this guy, Charlie, doesn't really smell very good. In fact, he kinda smells like a steaming pile of elephant shit.* I think for Michelle, our one and only encounter might've been a little too *Up Close & Personal.*

Later that year, Eddie and I were in New York City, and Eddie said, "Look, that's the set of *Brewster's Millions.* I wanna go talk to Richard Pryor."

On our way over to the set, I was talking about a badass martial-arts expert named Rashon who was Richard's bodyguard. I had already heard all sorts of stories about him, which had created a mysterious aura around the brother. The stories definitely built up my hope of one day crossing paths with this dude and getting to see what he was all about.

We got onto the set, walked onto a bus, and there sat Richard Pryor. I was trippin'. There was also another guy there, clean-shaven and dressed all in white like some James Bond character—white shoes, white socks, white fedora, white everything, perfectly pressed and creased. He was very serene, giving off a Fruit of Islam–type vibe. He looked at Eddie and me very casually, didn't say hello, then slowly turned his head to gaze back out the window. My immediate assumption was, *Here sits, in the flesh, the legendary, ass-whooping, karate expert extraordinaire Rashon*. I remember looking at him, thinking, *Wow. He must be good if he kicks ass wearing those white shoes.*

After our visit with Richard, I said to Eddie, "Yo, man, that other dude on the bus—that must've been Rashon."

"Rashon? *Shit*. That was Paul Mooney."

After that, I used to hear a lot about Paul Mooney and the stand-up material he was performing onstage. I went to one of his shows, and it was mind-blowing. I remember sitting there, listening to what he was saying, thinking that he was hilarious but that he could also make his audience very angry. I wondered how he managed to walk that line so well. I couldn't believe some of the things he said right to people's faces—and still made them laugh. What I eventually came to understand was that no-body else can do what Paul Mooney does. Period. That's his gift, his God-given talent. I instantly became a fan of his and have been to hundreds of his shows since.

Years later, when he opened for Eddie and we all went on the road together, my brother Vern and I used to torture the hell out of Paul Mooney. Our whole mission back then was to get a look at Paul's head without his ubiquitous skullcap. It's his signature affectation, and nobody ever sees him without it. Paul never, ever takes his hat off—no matter what. Vern and I used to dream up all sorts of Inspector Gadget hookups to separate Paul from his hat, or try to catch him under some remarkable circumstance when he wasn't wearing it.

One night we went so far as to pull the fire alarm in our hotel. We banged on Paul's door, yelling, "Fire! Fire! Everybody get out of the hotel!" Paul came out the door in his underwear.

Wearing his hat.

On the tour bus, poor Paul developed insomnia because he knew once he fell asleep we would do something like try to thread a fish hook into his hat and yank it off on a line.

I have nothing but love for Paul Mooney. He went out of his way to give me the opportunity to emcee his shows at Carolines so early in my career. That was a huge break for me. Even though I used every trick in the book to steal the hat off his bald head, Paul still had the class to help me fan the flame that has become my raging fire of desire to perform stand-up comedy.

. . .

In the mid-eighties, spending all that time traveling and hanging with Eddie and his celebrity friends and business associates, more so than meeting all the famous actors, singers, rappers, athletes, musicians, and comedians, I found that the people I always respected most were the fighters.

It probably goes back to the time I spent in the gym with Pop, and his love for the sport, but I count meeting professional boxers as one of the greatest blessings of the access Eddie's fame granted me in a world I would otherwise never have been a part of. It would be a long while before I began to discover what talents I might possess as a professional in the entertainment industry, so being with Eddie was the main reason those doors were open to me—and I took advantage of those opportunities every chance I got.

I got to meet and spend real time with Sugar Ray Leonard and Roberto Durán. I also met Marvelous Marvin Hagler in 1985 when he was on top of the world after successfully defending his title in three rounds against Thomas "The Hitman" Hearns. I also met Bernard Hopkins, and he has since come to one of my stand-up shows (as far as I'm concerned, that was the equivalent of Muhammad Ali coming to see me perform). These fighters were all the guys I had respected and admired for years. Getting to spend quality time with them was one of my great thrills during those first years home from the Navy.

Then a young kid fighting out of the Catskill Mountains in upstate New York started winning some big fights and rocketing up the rankings. His name was Mike Tyson.

I was a big fan of *Monday Night Fights* and I remember watching this young dude, originally from my hometown of Brooklyn, beating everybody about thirty seconds into every fight. I thought Tyson was incredible, and before long everybody else started to notice him, too.

Tyson was a fan of my brother's, so we had him over to the house in L.A. with two or three of his trainers. When we first met him, he was painfully shy. It was like watching a giant teddy bear—even though you knew that when that bear tore apart at the seams, a monster emerged. Before he was champ, Tyson would always talk about all the upcoming opponents he was afraid to fight. None of the people in the room could believe it. When Mike would start off saying, "Y'know who I'm afraid of . . . ?" I would think, *You better say God, motherfucker, because you can't be afraid of no man.*

That's the thing about meeting famous people outside of their public personas. I wasn't meeting their stage characters, I was meeting the real person, one-on-one. So yes, Mike Tyson was capable of being afraid. Knowing him the way I did, especially in the beginning, I can say he was no cold, emotionless killing machine. He felt fear every time he climbed between those ropes to face down an opponent. Tyson trained like a maniac and, in the beginning, he had unrivaled discipline. He also had a powerful belief in himself that every time he stepped into the ring, somebody was going to get thoroughly and completely thumped. And it was not going to be him.

Tyson started inviting us to his fights. We were in the crowd in 1986 when he fought Trevor Berbick for the heavyweight title. If you watch the footage of that bout, after Mills Lane calls the fight, Tyson goes to his corner, points over the ropes into the audience, and seems to say, *Whaddya think of that?* He was pointing at Eddie and our whole crew, cheering like crazy.

After he won the title, Tyson-mania exploded. We attended all his fights, and it seemed our friendship was growing closer. One day Mike drove over to the house in his new Bentley after he became the undisputed champion of the world. He gave a boxing lesson to Vern and me; he showed us how to deliver a blow that would rupture someone's bladder. Tyson said, in his little voice, "You gotta throw the punch at this angle. If he's been drinking water, let me tell you, there's gonna be a lotta problems."

But more than showing us what we could do inside a boxing ring, he gave us tips on how to keep ourselves safe in a street fight. He showed us punch combinations (Tyson used to use a number system created by his trainer, Kevin Rooney). His punches sounded like karate blows slicing through the air in some kung-fu movie.

Tyson was a good dude, and we spent a lot of time together up until he got married. Things changed after that. Mike was trying to live the life of a married man and his wife didn't want a bunch of pals (or, more often, sycophants) hanging around him all the time.

Tyson has lived a hard life with many twists and turns. He's been at the top, and he's seen the bottom, too. I can empathize with the brother. Choices I made in my life set me down some very destructive avenues until I got myself straightened out and focused again on what was important. Regardless of what people's personal opinions are of him today, Mike Tyson was a force of nature that I witnessed firsthand. Not since Muhammad Ali did a boxer get people as excited as he did.

Spending all that time on movie sets and hanging with Hollywood bigwigs started to make me feel self-conscious about being seen as just another member of Eddie's entourage, or worse, as some mooching family member. As Eddie's older brother, I've always had a sense of responsibility for him and have always protected him. Having people thinking of me as a hanger-on to his success was hurtful and made me question everything about myself, from my personality and talents to my very worth on the planet. I never believed I was just another member of Eddie's entourage. Nevertheless, I can't say I didn't enjoy the benefits of having a famous brother.

People in close proximity to a famous person can be nasty, and even though I knew in my heart that my motives were completely genuine, and that my brother could trust me above all others, a barrage of constant pettiness can start to wear a brother down.

In my private moments of reflection, I would think, *What do you mean, "entourage"? What do you mean, "hanger-on"? Are you trying to devalue my presence?*

But that's just the instinctive human response, especially when it comes to the people who surround a famous, and very wealthy, person. People angle selfishly for favor, riches, and power. When a person becomes as famous as Eddie, all the dynamics surrounding him change. It becomes very similar to a king and his court. His various courtiers are forever making strategic moves that they hope will maneuver them into the king's favor. And people like that, people who make those actions the main focus of their life, will cut your fucking throat in front of their own mother to stay in the king's good graces.

That's why when you're famous it's important to be extremely careful about who you allow to get close to you, because some people will exploit your relationship for their own purposes. We've all seen it happen to celebrities who abandon the real people who care about them (for instance, family and friends from home who have no qualms telling you you're an asshole). They go off and surround themselves with a new crew of make-believe jokers who, at the end of the day, only work to enrich themselves and cut off all challengers at the knees. Shit, that's the oldest story in Hollywood.

I'll always be proud of my brother because he never did that. He knew from his upbringing what sort of people he could trust and what sort of people he should do business with. Our father was a deliveryman and a transit cop, our pop was foreman at an ice cream factory, as well as a successful entrepreneur, and our mom was an operator for Bell telephone. All three were good people. Their common sense and common decency were handed down to me and my brothers when we went off to make it in the big, bad world. Now that I have achieved some measure of notoriety in the entertainment business, I try to apply the same honesty and integrity I was raised with to all my personal and business dealings.

Any integrity I have comes from Pop. He was a disciplined man who always dotted his *i*'s and crossed his *t*'s. *Discipline* was a big word that meant a lot in our house growing up. It doesn't only mean punishing someone for a transgression; discipline can also mean taking control of yourself—your words and your actions. Through many an ebb and flow in our individual lives—and in our relationships with one another—it's discipline that has guided me, Eddie, and our brother, Vern, into becoming the men we are today.

When I think about discipline, I think of hard work. And when I think about hard work, I also think about making sure I take time to play and enjoy life and have a good time. Otherwise, what am I working so hard to accomplish?

And when I think about having a good time, there's only one man who comes to mind: James Ambrose Johnson, Jr., of Buffalo, New York.

Better known as Rick James.

I met Rick because of Eddie's love of music. Rick had a studio in his house and invited us all to his compound in Buffalo while he and Kevin Johnson worked to produce Eddie's 1985 album, *Party All the Time*, the single for which hit number two on the Billboard charts. For a long stretch during the making of that album, we were snowed in at Rick's house in Buffalo, so all we did was party all the time. There you have it: art imitating life.

Rick's houses in Buffalo and L.A. were the bomb. There was Rick's house, and then there were, like, five other houses that surrounded it, all connected by tunnels. Every house had a different musical group staying inside, hanging out and partying, and there were girls everywhere. In the kitchen, Rick's chefs would cook you whatever you wanted, round the clock.

Rick was the first person I ever met who had a full swimming pool in his living room. He decorated his houses with exotic plants and live birds. I don't know anybody who didn't have fun hanging with Rick. He was the embodiment of joy.

Rick really respected Eddie, so through that connection we got the opportunity to spend a lot of time together, and we grew tight. Eddie used to call me "Rick James with No Money." I would go as far as to say that Rick became a member of the Murphy family. Rick was truly blessed with a rare talent to produce both music and fun. There's no one I've ever come across, before or since, who could even remotely touch his spirit.

Actually, there's a bit I do in my stand-up where I implore the audience to ease up on Britney Spears because I can see she's clearly possessed by the spirit of Rick James. I say that because only Rick, speaking through a vehicle like Britney, could say something like, "I'm going out to flash my pussy for the paparazzi. Keep the baby warm in the microwave; I'll be back in an hour, bitches."

Rick had a unique perspective on life. Absolutely nobody rolled like Rick. That was the era of the China Club on Seventy-fourth and Broadway in New York City, right next to the Beacon Theater in Manhattan. Every Monday night Rick would be there, along with the likes of Lawrence Taylor from the New York Giants and O. J. Simpson . . .

O. J. Simpson. Now there's a dude who should've dropped off everybody's radar while he was ahead. When you're an individual perceived to be the perpetrator of a notorious double homicide, disappearing from the scene is exactly the right move for you to make.

But not O.J.

Instead, we see him trying to shave a few strokes off his handicap out on the links, then he decides to assemble the Gang That Couldn't Shoot Straight, which looks more like a pack of broken-down zombies from *Night of the Living Dead,* and he shows up in Vegas to steal *his own football jersey*. As far as I'm concerned, that dude deserves to be where he ended up.

But there were all sorts of professional athletes hanging at the China Club back in those days, along with politicians, celebrities, captains of industry—you name it. It was a very odd mix because on one side of the club were all the celebrities, while on the other it was like the mafioso bar from *Goodfellas*.

It was like that scene where Ray Liotta is introducing every-body as he makes his way through the nightclub: "There was Anthony Stabile, Frankie Carbone, Mo Black's brother, Fat Andy, his guys Frankie the Wop, Freddie No-Nose, Pete the Killer (who was Sally Balls's brother), Nicky Eyes, Mikey Franscese, and Jimmy Two-Times, who said everything twice, like, 'I'm gonna go get the papers. Get the papers.' "

On the mob side of the China Club, the theme from *The God-father* played in your head. Meanwhile, on the other side of the wall, O. J. Simpson was poppin' disco moves on the dance floor.

I went to another club in Manhattan with Rick called Page Six. This club didn't even open till five o'clock in the morning. No place opens at that hour unless it's got music crankin' and everybody inside is wired up on blow.

You walked into this place and the ground floor was all mob-sters. One floor up was for gambling (poker, roulette, craps, et cetera); the next floor was a club with regular people just hang-ing out, dancing, and drinking; above that was a floor exclusively for gay people; and the top floor was designated for transgen-dered people.

This shit was all in one building!

Rick took me there and I said, "Yo, man! How the fuck did you find this place? I ain't never been to a place like this. This is debauchery central!"

Just as I expressed my elation and gratitude to Rick for tak-ing me there, the police busted in and raided the joint. They had a bus parked outside and were herding everybody out of the club.

As we left, one of the cops looked up and said, "Hey! That's Rick James! Go on, Rick. You're outta here."

He let us go. I'll never forget what a good feeling that was, to be rolling with Rick like that. Everybody else went to jail that night. I've had the good fortune to meet some extraordinary people over the years, and I have love for many of them, but I never bonded with anyone like I bonded with Rick James. He was one of a kind.

Speaking of one-of-a-kinds, my uncle Ray Murphy is my funniest uncle. When Eddie was honored by many of the country's movie theater owners at the 1986 American Cinematheque Ball, he brought along Uncle Ray and said, "Ladies and gentlemen, please welcome Uncle Ray! Get up here, Ray!"

Unfazed, Uncle Ray climbed onstage and did a few minutes of X-rated stand-up, peppering the audience with jokes like, "What about that bitch Whoopi Goldberg? Shit, she's ugly. If Whoopi wanted to go back with me to my hotel, I'd check into fifty rooms, turn out all the lights, and leave a note at the front desk saying, 'Find me, bitch.' "

Uncle Ray got a big laugh for that one. It was all in good fun. For my part, I have nothing but love and respect for Whoopi

Goldberg. I think she is the most talented female comedian I have ever seen onstage. She is one bad mamma jamma.

It's a funny thing, how inspiration can come from the unlikeliest of sources.

On one trip to the Bahamas, I found myself once again on a boat—this time with Eddie and the whole crew. Sitting on a deck chair a few paces behind me was Eddie's manager, Ritchie. I was standing at the rail, looking down at everybody swimming and having a good time in the water. Ritchie was talking with a buddy and I overheard the guy ask Ritchie, "And what does *that* one do? And what does *this* one do?" He was saying it just like that: "*That* one," like each person he pointed to wasn't a person at all—more like a function.

Then the dude arrived at me and said, "And his brother . . . What does *he* do?"

Ritchie said, "Him? He doesn't know what he wants. Just give him a warm-up suit and he'll be happy."

When I heard that, it cut right through me. I knew that if I spun around and challenged Ritchie on it, he would've squirmed and told me I misheard him. So I didn't say anything.

What I did instead was use that statement as fuel.

I don't know what I want? I'm the one who shouldn't be here? We'll see about that.

I have always believed that, at the end of the day, the one

who's left standing is the one who remains true to himself and true to those he loves. Over the years, I've met plenty of show-biz people who talked a good game, but for many of them, all of their words were just a never-ending fountain of horseshit. They eventually showed themselves to be frauds.

Despite the sentiment behind it, I knew there was a kernel of truth in what Ritchie was whispering behind my back. The question of who I was and what I was all about was haunting me, an issue I continued to avoid addressing. Time and again, I returned to the questions: *What is my gift? What do I have to share with the world? If I do have any special talents, clearly they're deeply buried. How can I coax them out to discover who Charlie Murphy really is?*

Me, doing kata, 1997.

My brother, Vern, and me with our sons,
Brandon, Charlie, and Kristofer, 1996.
We all stomped some ass that day!

CHAPTER SEVEN

WHO IS CHARLIE MURPHY?

After I had worked Eddie's security for a few years, the job had become fairly routine and I started contemplating my next move.

When I took a hard, honest look at myself and assessed what I considered my natural talents to be, my mind traveled straight back to first grade in Brooklyn and the one and only academic or artistic achievement I was ever recognized for: my writing. My essay, "What Brotherhood Means to Me," was not only my one shining intellectual moment in an otherwise physical childhood of underachievement, it was also an extraordinarily apt metaphor for the crisis I was going through—searching for my own identity away from the supernova that was my brother's fame.

I decided I would write a screenplay. I attended a three-day seminar put on by John Truby, a teacher who takes students through the whole process of writing a screenplay, step by step. He also offered instructional tapes that reinforced all the material he taught in his seminar. After I finished the seminar I read all the books on screenwriting I could get my hands on, including Syd Field's classic *Screenplay: The Foundations of Screenwriting* and *The Writer's Journey* by Christopher Vogler. I also talked with people who were successful at bringing their vision to the page and then getting it up on the big screen. I eventually reached a point where I was confident in the basics, such as how long a screenplay should be, how to structure a story in three acts, how to design and follow story and character arcs, why certain beats occur at certain points in a film script, and other technical aspects to the craft of writing. For instance, Truby taught us that there are only seven genres in film, and that every story ever told derives from some form of those core genres. After a lot of study and hard work in the art and process of screenwriting, I took a crack at my first script.

My first screenplay was titled *The Peddler*. I wrote it on legal pads, then transcribed it on a manual typewriter. In 1986, I sold it to Paramount Pictures for $150,000.

The process began when I decided I didn't want to write a story based purely in my imagination; instead, I wanted to research a true event that had never before been depicted. The biggest news story I remembered from growing up in New York was the ascent of the African American gangster Leroy "Nicky" Barnes. Barnes ran an all-black crime syndicate called The

Council, which controlled the heroin trade in Harlem from 1972 to 1983. His operation eventually grew to include all of New York State, as well as parts of Pennsylvania and Canada. Though The Council went on without him, in 1978, Barnes was convicted in a famous trial for drug trafficking and murder and was sentenced to life in prison without the possibility of parole. In 1998, Barnes was released into the Federal Witness Protection Program.

I went to the newspaper archives (known in newspaper parlance as "the morgue") of *The New York Times,* the *New York Post,* and the *Daily News* and pulled every article ever written about Nicky Barnes. This was before there was an Internet, so I had to do a lot of legwork the old-fashioned way. I gathered every word and photograph I could find. I read everything—*everything*—about Nicky Barnes's life, then structured it all into a screenplay.

I showed how Nicky went from being a drug addict to becoming a notorious drug kingpin with a cloak of invincibility around him. (In 1977 Barnes was pictured on the cover of *The New York Times Magazine* under the headline "Mr. Untouchable." Later, Barnes would use that as the title of his autobiography.) I thought it was an amazing story, a real hero's journey—even though the hero was a crook, which, admittedly, was very appealing to me.

When I sold the script, I believed very strongly that it would have been a remarkable role for Eddie to dig his teeth into. He, too, was fascinated by Barnes's story and was intrigued by the idea of playing against type. But the fortunes of Paramount Studios were riding on Eddie's shoulders, based on the success of the *Beverly Hills Cop* franchise. (The sequel, *Beverly Hills Cop II*, was filming at the time and would be released the next year.) I don't know what really happened, but I think they didn't want to do anything to tarnish Eddie's image with audiences by letting him play a bad guy—especially one who traffics heroin and murders people.

So Paramount stuck my script up on a shelf, where it remains to this day.

I thought, *Wow, man, I put all that work into writing that movie, and now it's never going to get made.*

I was sad about that, but when *New Jack City* was released in 1991, it made me feel a bit redeemed. I felt, at the very least, that I was on the correct path for writing something commercially viable. That movie, starring Wesley Snipes, Ice-T, and Chris Rock, and directed by Mario Van Peebles, was based on an original script titled *Nicky*, based on the life of Leroy Barnes. Much later, in 2007, Universal released *American Gangster*, starring Denzel Washington and directed by Ridley Scott, which is the *exact* story of Nicky Barnes. That film was nominated for a pair of Oscars and has grossed more than two hundred and fifty million dollars. I guess the idea of writing my first movie about Nicky Barnes was a good one. In a way, those movies getting made validated my writing and made me realize that the endeavor wasn't a total loss. I got paid good money for writing *The Peddler*, and I had confirmed to myself that the concepts I had for movies were in the right ballpark. Also, pouring myself into a new venture that was all my own, and showcasing talents no one ever knew I had, had filled me with a great sense of pride and satisfaction. It was another step along the road to discovering what Charlie Murphy was all about.

Getting a feature film made is a very difficult thing to do, so you must learn to measure your victories by a unique standard not immediately graspable in the normal workaday world. Very rarely do you have anything tangible to show for your enormous investment of time and effort. But the success of selling my first script inspired me to keep going. I was hungry to not only sell my work, but to go to a studio, pitch a concept, write it, get the budget, and see it up on the big screen.

In 1987, Keenen Ivory Wayans and Robert Townsend teamed up with Eddie to produce and direct Eddie's ninety-minute feature stand-up, *Raw*, at Madison Square Garden. After its release, *Raw*, the follow-up to *Delirious*, would go on to make more than fifty million dollars. *Raw* also had the notorious distinction of containing the most uses of the word *fuck* in a feature-length film until it was dethroned by *Goodfellas* in 1990. *Raw* was one of the greatest stand-up performances of all time and being there watching Eddie's flawless execution, is an experience I'll never forget.

A lot of the cats we would hang with back in the day, like Robert and Keenan, weren't celebrities yet; they were brothers on their way up, like Arsenio Hall (who would costar with Eddie in *Coming to America* the next year), and even Denzel Washington. I met all those dudes, and many more, long before they produced and directed movies, had their own TV shows, and were winning Oscars. It was fun to watch them growing into their careers and entertaining millions of people. I got to watch Arsenio blossom from doing stand-up in smoky little clubs on the Sunset Strip into becoming ArseniooOOOOoooo Hall.

Being around such creative, talented, and successful people all the time for so many years continued to inspire me. I didn't want to rest on the laurels of my success with *The Peddler*, so I started going out on acting auditions. One thing nobody can ever say about me is that I've achieved any of my goals through luck or nepotism. I have beat the street and been turned down a million times. I have heard, "No, not you," more than any one person should in the course of a single lifetime. Robert Guillaume once laughed in my face when I auditioned for a part on *Benson*.

One afternoon I strolled into the waiting room for a film audition, and there sat the ultimate Mr. Nice Guy comedian, Sinbad, wearing a purple jumpsuit with a matching pillbox hat. He was near the peak of his career at the time.

He said, "What up, brother? Listen, man, you go ahead and do your audition ahead of me. Go do your thing. Good luck."

I thought, *Hey, Sinbad's a cool dude. That's the way it should be—fellow actors supporting one another. After all, we're all in this together.*

I went into the audition, talked a minute with the producers, then took a quiet second to get my head straight before I started. In that moment, I realized I could hear every word being spoken outside in the waiting room. Sinbad had let me audition first so he could hear how I chose to read and how the producers reacted to it. With that thought clouding my mind, I proceeded to deliver what I still consider my worst audition ever. It was so horrible, I just said "Thank you" and left the room without waiting to hear what they had to say. It took poise and restraint to avoid having words with that jumpsuit-wearing motherfucker on my way back out to the elevator. But thanks for the lesson, Sinbad, because that's a trick I continue to use at auditions to this very day.

Acting is a tough gig. You need to have a strong belief in yourself to keep at it, and you need to be open to trying a lot of new stuff. I tell young people when I talk with them, including my son, who aspires to be an actor, that *no* will be the word you hear the most. You just need to find the strength inside yourself to stick it out. Then, when you finally hear *yes*, you have to take that opportunity and ride it hard, as hard as you possibly can. After you get that first yes, that's not the time to sit back and be mediocre or show up with a half-assed effort. When you get that all-important first yes, you need to work even harder than before. You need to convince yourself that you have the ability and the talent to reach the goals you set for yourself. That's why I worked on my writing harder than ever after selling my first script. And that's why, in spite of a tsunami of rejections at hundreds, if not thousands, of cattle calls—four auditions a day for six months—and sleeping on a friend's couch, I was determined to keep beating the streets until something broke in my acting career.

And finally, it did.

In 1988, I landed a role in a Stephen J. Cannell show starring Mario van Peebles called *Sonny Spoon*. I played Rat Man, a dude who had, according to my backstory, chewed off his own arm to escape from a Jamaican prison. He then swam in open ocean, with one arm, to freedom in the United States. Oh, and Rat Man didn't speak any English. Actually, he didn't speak. He just growled all the time.

Rat Man swam five hundred miles to America from Jamaica, with one arm.

The show was short-lived.

When I showed the tape to Eddie, he laughed hysterically through the whole thing.

At the time *Sonny Spoon* was gasping its last network breaths, my brother Vern and I were sharing a house, tinkering around with the idea of producing some hip-hop music together. I've always liked music, hip-hop was a new, up-and-coming genre, and Vern and I were just feeling out our abilities. I picked up a guitar and learned how to play it without any lessons. My brother Eddie did the same with guitar, piano, and drums.

Eddie's forays into music had also afforded me the opportunity to be in the studio with legends like Stevie Wonder and many other great recording artists of the era. I paid close attention to how they approached song structure. I learned that there are twelve bars of music, and how to write bridges, hooks, choruses, and verses. I wasn't just standing around holding the wall up; I was involved and alert in all my interactions with talented people. There was so much I could learn! I was soaking up all of the information I could from the greatest teachers in the world.

For a genius and worldwide megastar, Stevie Wonder is a very normal dude. I've known him for many years now and he is, without a doubt, one of my favorite humans on the planet.

Stevie is extraordinarily adjusted to his blindness. When you first meet him, your instinct is to try to help him do things, but he gets around just fine. You don't need to help Stevie do shit. (I've even seen him boxing. Yes, boxing. Pop would be proud.)

Stevie's studio is no rinky-dink joint. It's a large enough space for an entire orchestra to perform. We were in the studio, up for hours and hours, working on some tracks and grooving to the music, when Stevie suggested we wrap it up for the night and start again in the morning.

We were all leaving through the sound room, where there was a dude playing around with a Frisbee. The dude stood up, tossed the Frisbee all the way across the room, and Stevie Wonder caught it. Everybody kept walking out of the studio, acting like they hadn't just seen what they had seen. But it happened. That's the kind of shit that makes you question that brother's blindness.

Vern and I took what we learned from Stevie, the skills we

were developing on our own, and the advice and insight offered by music-industry professionals and artists we respected, and tried to produce some R & B and hip-hop. That led to the creation of the K-9 Posse.

The group featured the duo of Vernon "VAS" Lynch, Jr. (VAS stood for Versatile in Any Style) and his friend Wardell "Dubip" Mahone. Dubip's name was always a source of conversation. People would always ask him why his name was Dubip, and he would always come up with a new explanation. It had to be something new each time, because there's really no good reason why the dude's name should be Dubip. We made a demo and delivered it to our lawyer, Steve Barnes, who represented a lot of Motown artists out of L.A. He called us back within a few hours, and in less than a week he had secured us a record deal with Arista.

Suddenly I was part of the music game. K-9 Posse had a record deal, and now we had studio time to cut our first album. That was a fun time, going into the studio, staying up all night writing songs with a pad and pen, laying down tracks, producing a record, and trying to get it all just right. Eventually I had a studio set up in my house, with a soundboard and everything.

At that point in my life, everything was about trying to make a great record. K-9 Posse's debut album, *Ain't Nothing to It*, was released in 1988. It did well, selling more than three hundred thousand copies. We were in a good position to go gold with the next album, but we started having creative disagreements with the suits at Arista. The bottom line was, once we started butting heads with the record company, there wasn't much chance of us coming out with another good album. The creative process is a critical thing. If the artist is angry or irritated, it's like taking the tip of his pen and dulling it. Instead of his energy being sharp and focused on the task at hand—making great art—he starts to get frustrated, drawing with his dulled pen in wide, generic strokes. When are studio executives going to realize that the only time great art is created is when it has a unique voice? And the only way to encourage a unique voice is to leave a mother-fucker alone and let him do his thing.

The entire K-9 Posse experience lasted about three or four years. It was exciting for me to watch those dudes go from sitting around the crib talking about one day cutting an album to booking a world tour and performing on *Soul Train* and *The Arsenio Hall Show*.

In 1989 I got the opportunity to appear as Jimmy in Eddie's directorial debut, *Harlem Nights*—a movie he also wrote. In my humble opinion, *Harlem Nights* remains a classic of its genre. The story, the cinematography, everything about that movie was good. As a director, Eddie's choices were excellent.

What stands out most in my mind about shooting *Harlem Nights* is the time I got to spend with Redd Foxx. Getting to know Redd on a personal level was truly a thrill. I was blinded by the light on the set of that movie. There were Redd Foxx, Richard Pryor (who had released *See No Evil, Hear No Evil* the same year and was just starting to show signs of the illness that would eventually take his life), and Eddie, representing three generations of the best of American comedy. They were kings, and they all got together to do one film.

Richard Pryor was a comic god. It blows my mind that I got to work with him and act a scene with him. That's a moment and a memory that I treasure dearly. Oftentimes, the funniest shit Richard—and every other comedian—said on the set wouldn't make it into the movie. Richard and Redd were old friends, and watching them interact off-camera was priceless. When Eddie yelled "cut" and the crew started setting up for the next shot, that's when the real comedy began.

Once, when my childhood friend Woody was visiting L.A., I took him to the set to meet Redd Foxx. Woody is an excellent person, but somewhere along the line he let his front tooth rot. When he smiled, you saw this ugly black tooth with a yellow hole through it.

We rolled up to Redd's trailer and knocked on the door. I said, "Redd, this is my friend Woody. We grew up together."

Woody stuck his hand out, smiled, and . . .

Redd Foxx proceeded to launch into no less than forty-five minutes of A-rated comedy about Woody's rotten tooth. I was laughing so hard I can't even remember the jokes—not that I could do them any justice. Redd talked about Woody's tooth so mercilessly that after years of walking around with that funky mouth, Woody went straight to the dentist the next day and got it fixed.

• • •

In 1990, I played the role of Eggy in Spike Lee's *Mo' Better Blues*. With my writing, my acting, and my involvement in the music scene, I was starting to feel like I was carving out a career for myself.

I remember being on the beach in Malibu one afternoon at the house of producer Jeffrey Katzenberg, who began with *Who Framed Roger Rabbit?* and would later, as head of DreamWorks, team up with Eddie to work on the *Shrek* franchise.

I was standing on the balcony, looking down at a beautiful woman on the beach. She had her arms stretched wide and the wind was blowing through her long hair and her white, flowing dress as she walked toward the camera in a video shoot.

I said, "Who is that crazy bitch?"

The dude I was with was named Larry. He said, "That's Diana Ross."

"Get the fuck outta here. That ain't no Diana Ross."

Larry left and a little while later returned with Diana Ross. She took up her position on one side of the room with Katzenberg, Eddie, and all the other big movie people, while I hung out with the crew on the other side of the room. We were doing our thing and they were doing their thing.

We were talking, having a good time, listening to this dude Clint tell a very animated—and, as we might say in the Navy, salty—story filled with obscenities. Clint's short stature tended to give him a bit of a Napoleon complex, and he didn't take shit from anybody.

Suddenly Diana Ross stopped her conversation and crossed the room to where Clint was standing. She looked down and said, "Excuse me, I don't tolerate profanity in my presence."

Clint said, "What?"

"You heard me. If you want to use profanity, you're going to have to leave."

First of all, this wasn't even Diana's house. Second, we didn't work for her. Anyway, that's what we were all thinking, but we weren't going to say anything. That is, until Clint glared up at her and said, "Oh, really? You don't tolerate profanity in your presence? Well, *fuck you*, Diana."

After taking a few seconds to gather herself, Diana announced she was "appalled" and stormed out of the party. Clearly, Diana would not be adding Clint to her Christmas-card list that year.

In 1991 my second spec screenplay, *Campfire Stories*, which was a series of connected vignettes written in the spirit of *The Twilight Zone*, sold to Paramount for two hundred fifty thousand dollars. I was thrilled to be finding my stride as a writer and earning my own cash. Unfortunately, my script got shelved again and was never produced. That happens to a lot of stories, and to a lot of writers who pour their hearts and souls into every script they write. That's just Hollywood.

Meanwhile, I continued to book acting gigs. I performed the role of Livin' Large in *Jungle Fever*, which was released the following year, and that Christmas I was in a made-for-TV movie that we shot in Chicago called *The Kid Who Loved Christmas*. That was a great project because I got to play a jazz drummer named Jamal alongside some legendary African American performers. The incredible cast included the great Sammy Davis, Jr., Cicely Tyson, Ben Vereen, Ray Parker, Jr., Vanessa Williams, Esther Rolle, and Della Reese.

Sammy's cancer was far along at that stage. He was on death's doorstep and in tremendous pain. A weaker person would've stayed home, but Sammy was the ultimate professional. He showed up to work every day, fully committed to doing his job. I learned a lot about what it means to be a man by watching how Sammy conducted himself on the set of that film. Sammy loved his work, and his work was his life. He was determined to perform to the very end.

Cicely, Della, and Esther were like the gang of three on that project—the grandes dames of black actresses. I remember watching them perform a scene together where they were chasing the kid, played by Trent Cameron, down the steps into the subway. Trent played Reggie and was about ten years old, while Cicely and Della were in their late fifties and Esther was nearly seventy.

The director, Art Seidelman, shot the scene with all three ladies bounding down the stairs after Trent at full speed, then he yelled, "Cut! Back to one!" which means everyone needs to get back to their first positions for another take. Mind you, this wasn't some normal set of steps they were running down—this was a tall, wide staircase descending into Chicago's main train terminal.

After Art had them go back and do it a third time, Della Reese went up to him and said, "If you say 'back to one' one more time, I think the three of us are gonna have to put a whoopin' on you."

Della was not joking. Art decided that he had the shot and they moved on to the next setup.

Despite the stellar cast, the most outstanding memory I have of that entire production didn't occur on the set. One day I was in the chair talking up the makeup girl, who was white. Making small talk, I said, "I'm gonna be out here in Chicago for a while. Where do you go to hang out?"

"A few different places."

"Yeah? Well, where are you going Saturday night?"

"A place called Neo's."

"Really? Where's Neo's? Because if you're going to be down there on Saturday, maybe I can meet you there."

She said, "If you want to meet me at Neo's, you're more than welcome."

Saturday rolled around and I hailed a cab in front my hotel and said, "Take me to Neo's."

I started to get uneasy as the cab drove a half-hour away from downtown Chicago. I'm from New York; a half-hour away from my hotel in a strange city leaves me completely lost. Eventually the driver pulled up to the end of a long, dark alley and said, "The place you want to go to is at the end of that alley."

"Say what?"

From the cab, I looked down toward the other end of the alley and, lo and behold, there was a little red neon sign that read NEO'S hanging over a steel door. I paid the driver and, as I made my way down the alley, I began to hear the faint *boof-boof-boof* of dance music coming from inside the club. I knocked on the door. It opened.

Standing just inside was a bald, white bouncer. I glanced beyond his tattooed shoulder and caught a glimpse of the all-white crowd, throwing themselves against one another in a crazed mosh pit to the sound of death metal and realized the makeup chick had lured me to a skinhead bar.

The bouncer said, "What do you want?"

"Uhh, I thought I was supposed to be meeting someone here, but I guess I was wrong."

"We don't want people like you in here."

"Totally understandable. Have a good evening."

As I walked back toward the street, the alley felt like it had been extended by a half-mile. I could feel the hateful energy pounding against the other side of that steel door like that angry wave that almost swept me off the deck of the USS *Joseph Hewes* the night those racist hillbillies tried to make me take out the garbage in a storm.

I walked away from Neo's at a good pace as two thoughts ran through my mind: *(1) How the fuck am I gonna find another cab outta here?* and *(2) That bouncer is probably in there right now saying, "Hey! Everybody! Some nigger just tried to come in!"*

Sure enough, over my shoulder I heard, "Hey, nigger!"

Oh, no, I thought. *It's about to go down.*

I turned to look and—

Remember the TV show *Laugh-In*? There was a dude named Arte Johnson who played a German soldier named Wolfgang who hid behind a bush, spying on the show, and would always say in a thick accent, "Very interesting." This dude who ran out after me looked exactly like Arte Johnson's little German soldier—including his little Nazi helmet.

He said, "Where you going, nigger?"

I kept walking toward the street, but now that I saw it was just some goofy dude coming after me all alone, I felt a lot less nervous about the situation. As I neared the end of the alley, Little Adolf started goose-stepping faster, trying to catch up.

I wheeled around and said, "Look, man, you better stop following me."

"Nigger, I wanna know what made you think you were coming into Neo's tonight. *Nigger.*"

I kept walking. When I hit the street, I saw a taxi barreling right toward me, and I hailed it. I turned again. Now he was right behind me.

So I dropped him with one punch.

I wasn't going to wait to see what he was planning to do. For all I knew, he might have pulled a vintage Luger out of his ass and shot me. I jumped in the cab and saw that the driver was a black dude.

He shook his head and said, "See? That's what happens when you try to hang with the white folk."

Speaking of white folk—or almost-white folk, at any rate—in 1991, during the filming of the video for his hit "Remember the Time," directed by John Singleton, in which my brother played a pharaoh with the model Iman as his queen, I finally got the opportunity to meet the real Michael Jackson, not just a Hollywood impersonator.

I grew up admiring Michael and listening to his music, but when he started changing, I was one of the few people in my crew saying, "What the fuck is going on with that brother?" Everyone around me kept acting like he was perfectly normal, but I said, "No, no. Something is seriously fucked up with that dude."

"Well," they said, "Michael is just different."

"He's different, all right. My man went from being the King of Pop to the Phantom of the Opera."

I went to meet Michael in his trailer. The interior was designed to look like a mystical, magical circus trailer from some old-time movie. It was filled with mannequins, drapery, and a host of other bizarre oddities. It was dark in there, too, and when I peeked in, Webster—Emmanuel Lewis, that is—was sitting cross-legged on a table. I watched Michael just sitting there, gazing at himself in the mirror.

It was so weird, I thought, *You know what? I don't really need to meet Michael Jackson that bad after all.*

Despite my feelings about him, I was shocked when Michael died. He went way before his time. I don't believe that his contributions to music and popular culture can ever be equaled. Michael was one hundred percent consumed by show business, on and off the stage. They say Elvis was the King of Rock 'n' Roll and Michael was the King of Pop. At least Elvis remained one color throughout his life. We'll never again see the likes of Michael Jackson and we'll never again see another artist who was born black and died paper white.

Later that same year, I was with Eddie in Washington, D.C., while he was shooting *The Distinguished Gentleman*. On the set there was a large, affable boom operator who kept cracking jokes, entertaining the cast and crew. His name was Paul Farmer and we told him that he was a naturally funny dude and should seriously consider a career as a stand-up comic.

As fate would have it, our paths would cross more than once after that encounter, and today Paul Farmer, aka Freez Luv, is my opener whenever and wherever I perform my stand-up comedy. Freez has been on the road with me since 2006, and also collaborates with me on projects like *Charlie Murphy's Crash Comedy* on the Crackle Network for Sony.

After leaving *The Distinguished Gentleman* set one day, Eddie and I were sitting in a hotel room together, trying to brainstorm new feature film projects that would be different and urban, but at the same time would cross over to a wide audience. We started with the thought that vampires are sexy to everybody, so we got the idea to take vampires and drop them in the 'hood. That's where the seed that would eventually grow into the film *Vampire in Brooklyn* was planted.

Eddie said, "That's a great idea, man. We're gonna write that."

We began to do a ton of research on vampires. I outlined the story on legal pads, and then we wrote the script. It would be a few years before that seed of an idea came to fruition, but, after all the study and hard work I'd devoted to my screenwriting, *Vampire in Brooklyn* would turn out to be my first feature film that made it to the big screen.

Unfortunately, it was during this time, lasting for a period of about three years, that Eddie and I had a falling out and didn't speak to each other. It all started, as with most arguments between family, with some trivial shit. I don't even recall what we were fighting about, but the exchange escalated into an all-out argument. It was the first time that we had ever confronted each other so aggressively as adults. I refused to back down, and he wasn't going to back down, either.

What I forgot to take into account was that I was engaging

in an argument in Eddie's environment, on his home turf. Therefore, regardless of the issue, I was wrong and he was right.

I'll admit that stubbornness is one of my character defects. In the end, it was me who walked away and refused to be the first to apologize and repair the damage. Now I realize the whole situation resulted from ignorance, and I regret it. Life is too damn short to hold on to petty shit like that.

It was during this period of estrangement from Eddie that Vern came over to my house and showed me how he could drag our friend Andre across the floor by one of his fingers.

I asked Vern, "What is that?"

He said, "It's called a finger lock."

"Finger lock? I wanna learn that shit. How did you learn it?"

"Karate."

Back in the early seventies, when we had just moved to Roosevelt and movies like *Five Fingers of Death* and Bruce Lee's *Enter the Dragon* played at the Nassau Theater, Eddie and I caught kung-fu fever.

After seeing the all-time classic *Seven Samurai*, we decided to break branches off of trees and have samurai sword fights. Friends of mine named Rich Stevens and Frankie Rivera got into it good one afternoon. Their branches got tangled, and when Rich jerked his back, Frankie's stick flew into Rich's eye and poked it out. Rich was a tough dude. He picked up his eyeball and said, "Can somebody please take me home?" He lost his eye, but it was all for the love of the fists of fury.

Around that same time Eddie started doing a great Bruce Lee impression and enjoyed busting it out during his karate lessons. Eddie talked, moved, kicked, and twirled nunchakus just like Bruce. Even today, if you watch Eddie on-screen, I think you can still see a Bruce Lee vibe coming off of him. I think Bruce got into his blood.

We used to work on our karate technique in the basement. Being the older brother, I played the role of teacher, even though I had no clue what I was doing. One day I was showing Eddie what I thought was a side kick. I said, "You do it like *this*."

Eddie said, "No, you do it like *this*," then he put his foot through the Sheetrock wall.

I said, "Pop is going to kill you for this."

I came up with the idea of dragging our giant floor-model television five feet to the left so it covered up the hole. For the next four months, Pop, who watched television almost every night, never noticed. Every night, Eddie and I sat with Pop in the basement, holding our breath. When he finally discovered the hole, I told him what had happened. Pop determined that the statute of limitations had run out and granted us both leniency.

For a while, I took karate lessons at a dojo under a sensei named Fabian Williams. But, as with boxing, the regimentation of the study spoiled my interest. Again, I had energy without focus. It would be many years before I regained my interest and returned to the balance and discipline of karate.

There was a karate dojo in Ringwood, New Jersey, that I drove past for years. It always had paper taped up, covering all the windows. I would often wonder what wondrous feats of controlled violence were going on inside, behind all that paper. So finally, one day in 1992, after Vern's finger-lock display, I stopped to peek inside. This dude jumped out and said, "Whaddya want?"

I said, "I wanna join."

His name was Keenan Winterfield. He took me inside to his office and sat me down. He said, "Classes are Monday, Wednesday, and Friday for adults. Today's Wednesday. Wednesday is fight night, so you can't come. You'll start on Friday."

When I arrived on Friday, Keenan had already told the whole class that Eddie Murphy's brother, a wannabe tough guy from the movies, was joining their dojo. Every dude in that joint couldn't wait to fuck me up the first chance he got.

For the next few weeks, we started to get to know one another as the members of the dojo showed me the various stances, punches, and kicks. Everyone just seemed to be going through the motions with me; they weren't really willing yet to accept me as one of their friends.

I was going home after every class thinking, *I can't wait to start sparring. I'm gonna whup some ass. I'm gonna fuck everybody up and shoot right from white belt all the way to black belt.*

I was really thinking that. After four weeks of training, exercise, running, jumping jacks, and all the other conditioning, they told me I was fighting on Saturday and to show up with all my pads.

Saturday rolled around and I was in my car driving to the dojo. Suddenly I started questioning how prepared I really was for my first karate fight since junior high. I thought, *Nobody has specifically told me what I need to do in a match. Here I am, in my mid-thirties, driving to go get into a karate fight. You sure you want this, bro?*

I decided I had to do it. I was already committed; I'd bought the equipment; I'd been talking big about it. I had to follow through. I got there and suited up in my uniform and pads.

They said, "Murphy, you're going to be fighting this guy right here."

His name was Big Terrance, and it wasn't an ironic nickname. Terrance was young—maybe twenty-two—and a former football player who weighed about 225 pounds but was quick and agile. Big Terrance was probably the meanest possible guy for me to spar against.

While I was considering this, Keenan Winterfield screamed, "Begin!"

I didn't know the first thing about formal sparring. I knew how to hold my hands up and throw jabs in a boxing match, and I sort of knew how to throw some kicks, but I hadn't thrown a kick at a human being in longer than I wanted to remember. The one kick I thought I had down pretty well was a roundhouse.

That was my go-to move. I came right out and threw a hard roundhouse at Big Terrance.

He blocked it.

I thought, *Well, there's my whole arsenal. What's next?*

What's next was Big Terrance jumping in the air, throwing hook kicks, side kicks, back kicks, back fists, overhands, and uppercuts.

What the fuck?

Big Terrance beat the shit out of me. At one point, he kicked me in my nose so hard I was positive it was broken. The heel of his foot smashed the center of my face like an RTV bus. The sides of my nose felt like they'd splashed past both my ears. And it wasn't just me who thought it was broken—everybody in the dojo jumped up to ask if I was okay.

I said, "It ain't bleeding, so let's keep fighting."

That was the moment that finally broke the ice with the other members; that's when I officially became a part of the dojo. They respected me because I didn't quit. Later in the day, while I was licking my wounds (luckily, my nose was not broken), some members gathered around.

One said, "We understand your brother is Eddie Murphy."

"He is."

"Well, we just wanted you to know, we don't give a shit who your brother is. We're still gonna whip your ass, just like we did today. Come back next week, and we'll whip it all over again."

"Really?"

"Yeah, really."

"Okay. I guess I'll see you next week."

Every Saturday for a year I was like a human punching bag. But after that first year, I stopped coming home every night all lumps and bumps, wrapped in ice and Ace bandages. The fear of getting beat down motivated me to work hard and keep improving. I started to learn how to defend myself. And I started to appreciate not just the physical, but also the mental benefits of devoting my energy to karate.

I walked into Winterfield's Martial Arts during a rough patch in my life, having lost touch with my brother and with many of the things I had worked hard to accomplish. Devoting myself to karate and losing myself in its demands and discipline gave me the focus I needed to get my life back on track. My decision to stop and peek into that dojo had come at the perfect time in my life, when I was open and ready to accept the challenges that karate presented, and the clarity it would provide as I applied its principles to my relationships and my career. Since that first day, I went on to become one of the top fighters in the dojo, earning my black belt. I remain an active member today.

One of the reasons I've stuck with karate is because of the type of people I've made friends with by staying involved with it. They're the kind of people that you want your kids to meet and look up to as positive role models. The men I train with are all honorable, with good jobs as police officers, FBI agents, soldiers, and stockbrokers on Wall Street. There are plenty of characters in the world. It's a lot harder to find people *with* character.

Karate has helped me round out the lessons of discipline that Pop began teaching me so many years ago. Belonging to a dojo has also been a great source of camaraderie for me. It reminds me of my dedication to the unit that was instilled in me at boot camp and throughout my six years in the service. And to a large extent, it also reminds me of the spirit of fellowship I share with other comedians, whether we're on the road together or just hanging out, telling war stories, and trying to one-up each other in the greenroom before a show.

Sometimes I get beat down—in a sparring match, or in my personal or professional life. But I've learned time and again that the only way to improve is to get up and keep moving forward.

Karate taught me that, in a lot of situations, there's going to be a cloudy period before everything becomes crystal clear. In comedy, during that cloudy period at the beginning of my stand-up career, I started with very primitive material—corny, even. I did whatever I could to get the crowd laughing. But I focused on breaking down my performances and improving one key element at a time—having a more commanding stage presence, or making better eye contact—until I could develop better jokes and graduate to more mature material.

It's the same thing with karate. The focus isn't all about kicking somebody's ass. It can't be. It's about taking control of yourself and learning how to use whatever skills you possess at that moment.

Things that aren't important tend to fall naturally to the

wayside as you sharpen your focus on what it is you really want. I know there are tons of people in this world with more talent than me in every field I've pursued, but hard work, tenacity, and seizing moments when they have been presented to me are what have always led me to good things. The best things.

On the set of *Bar Starz*, 2005.

Kimbo Slice before he went bald.

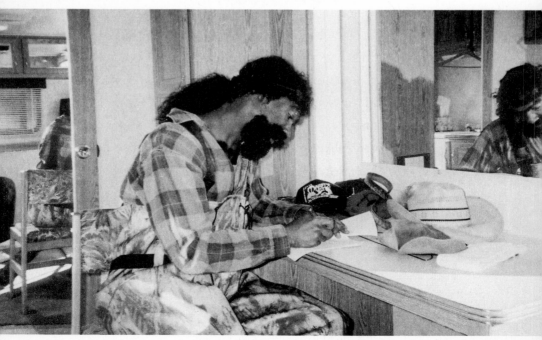

CHAPTER EIGHT

BREAKTHROUGH

My feud with Eddie concluded in a much less climactic fashion than it began. I was hanging in a club in New York and I watched Eddie walk past me. We hadn't spoken in three years, but I broke the ice and said, "Wassup?"

"Yo. Wassup."

And that was it. The great Murphy feud was over, and we were back to kickin' it together. It goes back to principles I seemed to have understood instinctively as a kid when I wrote "What Brotherhood Means to Me." I love my brothers, Eddie and Vern. In life there are always going to be conflicts—you mix it up, you work it out, you move on. But you can't waste those moments. You have to learn from them and figure out which aspects you can use to make yourself a better person. I'll freely admit that my life has always been, and still is, a work in progress.

Along the way, a few good things started happening for me. The first was my breakout role as Gusto in the 1993 film *CB4*, which was way before its time and has since become a cult classic. Chris Rock called me up one day and said, "Charlie, I'd like you to come down and audition for a character. I think you'd be real good."

I said, "What's the role?"

"Don't worry. All you gotta do is come in and act mean. *Real* mean."

I went down and read for the audition. They seemed to like my performance. Chris said, "That was great, Charlie. Now come back tomorrow, and act even meaner."

"Meaner?"

"Oh, yeah, as mean as you can get."

"Okay."

So the next day I went down to the audition with a loaded 9mm. I acted the scene—literally foaming at the mouth—then pulled out the 9mm and popped in the clip. Now even I know that's fucking insane. Actors don't get roles that way. In fact, I want anyone reading this to know: Don't ever try that. I was in fucking outer space when I did that shit. However, they *did* give me the role. You never see Gusto foaming at the mouth in a single scene of *CB4*, but that's the direction Chris Rock gave me for my audition. And it worked.

The next year, for the first time in my career as a screenwriter, the green light finally flashed and a movie I wrote was going to be made. Paramount picked up *Vampire in Brooklyn*, the concept Eddie and I started to develop while he was filming *The Distinguished Gentleman*. The film would star Eddie and Angela Bassett, and horror master Wes Craven was signed on to direct.

That was a tremendous feeling of accomplishment. I considered all the things I had worked hard writing that had never sold, and I considered all the scripts I'd written that had sold but never been made. I was on top of the world. I'm very proud of how that film turned out, and I'm proud that my name is on it. Every now and then, I'll see it on TV and I'll watch some, or all, of it. I love knowing that I was a part of making something that, years later, is still part of the culture of entertainment.

When you think about it, Eddie has never played a villain except in *Vampire in Brooklyn*. When it premiered in 1995, *Vampire in Brooklyn* was panned by the critics, but I didn't care. I was just happy to see it made. And there was always something odd that stuck in my mind about that whole experience: When I bought a ticket at my local theater, my stub said *Ace Ventura: Pet Detective*. As far as I'm concerned, that was not an isolated incident. Call me nuts, or a conspiracy theorist, or whatever, but I'll always be skeptical of the official box office records for *Vampire in Brooklyn*.

After the film debuted, I went back to working long hours writing spec scripts and pitches. I thought I'd get offers for paid writing assignments after I earned my first feature film credit, but it didn't work out like that for me. After a while, it seemed I wasn't getting anywhere with my writing, and I lost my drive and motivation. Writing wasn't fun anymore and I started to feel like I was no longer writing with a purpose.

Luckily, acting opportunities kept popping up. In 1995 I appeared in the video short *Murder Was the Case*, a project I did with Snoop Dogg. I got that role because Snoop and Dr. Dre were fans of my performance as Gusto in *CB4*. On the set of that shoot, I crossed paths again with Freez Luv (aka Paul Farmer), who had taken our advice and gone on the road with a successful stand-up comedy act. Freez and I really hit it off and started to form the relationship that has blossomed into the tight friendship we have today.

For several years I bounced around, acting here and there, and writing. I played Saxaphone Man in *The Pompatus of Love* with Jon Cryer and Kristin Scott Thomas. That was one of the few roles I ever received as the direct result of an audition. I think what won me the role was that I convinced the director, Ritchie Schenkman, that I was crazy. Not anywhere near as crazy as my Gusto audition for Chris Rock, but authentically crazy (as opposed to just acting crazy).

In that film there's a scene where my character goes over the edge of the roof of a four-story building and hangs and spins by the tail of his jacket before being pulled up. To set up the shot, they raised me up on a scaffold, tied me to a harness suspended from the roof, then took the scaffold away. When I looked down, I knew that if the line or harness snapped I would be dead, but when we shot the scene, I didn't hold back—I flailed and struggled in the air like a wild man. When they had the shot, they raised the scaffold back up, unhooked the harness, and brought me back down to street level. I stepped off the scaffold and an actress said to me, "You know you didn't have to do that, right?"

"What're you talking about?"

"There are SAG rules. Our union contract states that we don't have to get on anything over three feet high. They have to get a stuntman for that. You just risked your life for how much money?"

I said, "This would have been a great conversation for us to have before I shot that scene."

In 1998, Ice Cube had me play a dude named Brooklyn in *The Players Club*. He called me up when I was with Eddie on the set of *Metro* and said he was making a movie and wanted me in it. I found myself in the company of great actors who were still on their way up, like Jamie Foxx, Terrence Howard, and Bernie Mac. Those guys all went on to accomplish great things after that project.

As far as my film-acting career goes, *The Players Club, Harlem Nights, Vampire in Brooklyn, Mo' Better Blues*, and *Jungle Fever* are movies I see playing on television all the time. That's something I take pride in because I know that's not always the case—even when you're very happy with your performance in a film. You don't have much control over what will become popular with audiences and what will fade and be forgotten.

When I say that hard work always leads to good things, I

mean that literally. I was on the floor in my dojo, stretching and chatting with one of the dudes I trained with, when he told me that Jay-Z's partner, Damon Dash, was making movies and that he was looking for writers.

He said, "He may be interested in hiring you. You want me to get you a meeting?"

I hadn't been focusing on my screenwriting as much since becoming so disillusioned after *Vampire in Brooklyn*, but I was excited by the prospect of getting back into it. The next day I sat down for a meeting with Damon Dash at Roc-A-Fella Records. It was a crazy meeting. We were sitting there having a serious conversation about me writing a film for his company, and there were thirty other people in the room. We hit it off and Damon hired me to write the film *Paper Soldiers*, which was released on DVD in 2002.

But more than anything I will always remember 2002 as the year Pop died. When we learned Pop had lung cancer, it was like we *all* had lung cancer. Pop dealt with it like the prizefighter he was, though—all the way to the end. Throughout his battle, he never felt sorry for himself and never allowed us to feel sorry for him. When he passed, his funeral service was the polar opposite of my dad's. It was a closed-casket ceremony with Pop's photo placed on top. People showed respect for his integrity and accomplishments by acting with decorum and class at his funeral.

Pop's memory remains very strong in my heart and mind. Even now, I find it difficult to welcome anyone Mom is dating.

People say, "Whaddya mean? Your mother is in her sixties."

My answer is, "Exactly. So why is she dating?"

When I think about Mom showing up at my door upset over some dude, the next thing I think about is how I'm gonna have to kill him. I think both my brothers are on the same page with that. Pop was it. Now Pop's gone. No dating. There is no *next dude*. We will probably never accept another guy. That's sad for Mom, but that's just how it is. Vernon Lynch, Sr., was it—there can never be another Pop.

In 2003 I was home on my couch, watching TV with the sound off, when the phone rang. My business manager, who also represented Dave Chappelle, said, "Charlie, Dave has a new show coming out on Comedy Central called *Chappelle's Show*. They'd like you to come down to play a part in one of their sketches."

I called and spoke with Neal Brennan. He described the role of an ex-con named Tyree, who had been cast in a show called *The Mad Real World*. The concept for the bit was based on all those reality shows, starting with MTV's *The Real World*, that feature a group of angst-ridden Caucasians housed with one, maybe two, African Americans. In all those shows, if there is a male black dude, he's immediately labeled as the angry, unstable one in the house. *Chappelle's Show* wanted to turn that whole concept on its head by creating a token white dude (played by comedian Christian Finnegan) in a house where he was surrounded by legitimately dangerous and crazy black folk who berate and humiliate him mercilessly—including my boy, Lysol, just home from the joint, who bangs Christian's TV girlfriend while he watches, masturbating and crying.

I could see right away that this was not going to be the normal TV fare. The thing I remember most about that first assignment on *Chappelle's Show* was that it felt like a family of sharp-minded, witty people working together to create some genuinely hilarious, forward-thinking material. It appeared that their mission was to dance like nobody was watching and let the chips fall where they may. The Mad Real World episode wound up being the top-rated show of season one

The show was still very new when I got there, so the vibe behind the scenes felt wide open. Anybody could approach Dave with a sketch idea. That's how I was able to get a few of my ideas produced. With the wrong combination of people on a television show, it can be aggravating for the writers and producers to deal with actors constantly pitching ideas to them. I was lucky to fit in enough that I could present my concepts in a fashion that didn't piss anybody off—usually in the cafeteria during meals.

Neal Brennan was always available to listen to ideas. He appreciated the creative process and would always talk with me. Between Dave and Neal, Neal is the one who would meet me in pubs for a beer to kick around ideas.

Dave was accessible, but he could also be very inaccessible at the same time. He was always friendly and hung with all the people who created the show, but like most people who live mainly in their own heads, he picked his moments. As we all know now, as the show became a runaway hit (and a huge moneymaker) for the network, Dave came under increasing pressure from all sides, and he carried a lot of that weight, rightly or wrongly, on his own shoulders. In the end, I guess the pressure just got to be too much. I can't really say what happened for sure because I never asked Dave why he left the show when it was at its height. Though I love Dave (how can anybody not love Dave?), he was always guarded and protective of his privacy, so I never felt that we were close.

Sometimes, Dave would just vanish.

But I'm the type of person who avoids discussing anything that might make a person uncomfortable. If I meet you and you have a nub at the end of your arm where a hand should be, and you don't mention anything about it, I'm not going to ask. It's not my nub.

That whole first season, I made the Screen Actors Guild minimum for each of my appearances. I remember somebody saying to me back then, "Yo, man, you're on *Chappelle's Show* and you're only getting five hundred bucks an episode? You're a chump, man. They're robbing you!"

I said, "Well, you know what? I'm just gonna have to be a chump and get robbed, because I'm on national television every week. And that, to me, is priceless."

I can recall a number of comedians who had golden opportunities working on that show but quit because they were pissed off about the money. I believe that hard work always leads to more work and new opportunities. It opens doors that you never knew would be available for you to step through. I was looking at the big picture during my time on *Chappelle's Show*. I didn't care that I wasn't making a million dollars, and I had no idea what my next move might turn out to be, but I knew I had a shot to blow up every week on one of the hottest shows on TV. That was more than enough for me.

If Dave had decided to stick around, I think we all would've started making some serious money. But it was what it was. In 2006, Donnell Rawlings and I hosted what Comedy Central dubbed "The Lost Episodes" of *Chappelle's Show*. They were composed of the sketches and bits and pieces of season three that were already in the can when Dave walked.

Why did we host the show? Why not? It was a gig, and Dave never asked us not to.

Except for the show ending prematurely, I consider my entire experience working on *Chappelle's Show* to be a positive one. Ultimately, it's led to my career doing stand-up and finding a deep and abiding passion for a form of entertainment I had no realistic expectation of coming to—let alone succeeding at—at the age of forty-two. As far as the dustup over how *Chappelle's*

Show ended, I have nothing to complain about—in fact, the way things worked out for me, the only thing I feel about it is gratitude.

Now, if you spend any time with me, you quickly learn that I communicate my experiences by recounting stories. So, one afternoon, backstage at *Chappelle's Show*, we were at the table eating lunch. I was talking, telling stories from back in the day, about how I got bitch-slapped by Rick James, which ignited my ghetto side, forcing me to get back at him. Everybody was laughing, and Dave said, "This shit's real, man. We gotta make this into a sketch."

I said, "This ain't a sketch. This shit's my life."

After lunch I had a meeting with Neal Brennan, a couple of other dudes, and an actress. I retold the Rick James story for all of them and then left while everybody in the room was still laughing. The actress came up to me afterward and said, "You're going to let them make a sketch out of that?"

"Yeah. Why not? It all happened."

"You're crazy."

I didn't see what the problem was. I knew Rick himself would vouch for it (and he did, hilariously). So I sat down and wrote out the first Rick James sketch, where Rick and I hook up at the club for the first time, in the VIP room. Neal gave my script a rewrite, and then we shot it. The exasperation in the straight-man delivery I use in those segments is all the result of Neal's direction. Neal gave me the same advice he would later offer before I took the stage for my first stand-up set at the Laugh Factory: "Charlie, don't try to be funny. Just tell the story like you were telling it at the lunch table. Be yourself."

I gave Dave a brief lesson on how Rick talked and walked, and some of his other mannerisms. Dave had Rick down cold in about five minutes. But that's just a testament to Dave's amazing talent. The classic punch lines and throwaway lines attributed to Rick James in those sketches are mostly the product of the improvisational genius of Dave Chappelle.

"It's a celebration!"

"I wish I had more hands so I could give them titties four thumbs down!"

"It's the stickiest of the icky!"

"I'm Rick James, bitch! Enjoy yourselves."

When we wrapped shooting, I was very pleased with the final cuts of the Rick James segments. I thought they were very well-edited and very funny. But still, I was nervous about how the audience would react to these twenty-five-year-old stories about an R & B funk musician that many younger audience members might not even be familiar with. I would just have to wait and see.

Right before the first screening, Donnell tapped me on the shoulder and said, "Charlie, you don't understand what's about to happen, do you?"

"What do you mean?"

"That sketch is the bomb, brother. It's gonna make you famous."

I wasn't thinking about fame. I was just looking for a few laughs, a bit of public acceptance, and the guarantee of more roles. I was forever locked in the mentality of scratching and clawing for more work.

I was in a soundproof room when they fired up the sketch for the live studio audience. When they watched Rick/Dave slap me in the face, then saw me throwing Rick/Dave into a mirror in super slow-mo, and then listened to Rick James himself chuckling and admitting to the world that "cocaine's a hell of a drug," I was either in a very poorly constructed soundproof room or the laughter was so uproarious that no walls could contain it. I couldn't believe my ears. But there it was.

It wasn't long before everyone involved with *Chappelle's Show* started to realize how popular those sketches had become. The first one went viral on the Internet almost instantly, and it seemed like absolutely everyone was talking about it. When I saw some dude on TV at the NBA play-offs running up and down the court with a big sign that read I'M RICK JAMES, BITCH! I thought, *Goddamn right. It's a celebration, bitches!*

The week that first Rick James sketch blew up, in the winter of 2004, was the same week I found myself seated beside Donnell, who was calling me out, telling the listening audience of *The KISS 98.7 Wake-Up Club* in New York City that I was afraid to step to a microphone and perform stand-up comedy.

That challenge is what led to my awkward, but otherwise enjoyable, first-ever stand-up act at the Laugh Factory in front of Donnell, Neal, Rob Stapleton, and a gracious audience of about one hundred people. That small success, and the persistence of Neal and Donnell, lit a fire that burned so hot in my belly I went straight out on the road for the "I'm Rich Bitch" tour before I even had a full stage act. One performance at a time, I improved until Mike Epps hired me to open for him.

Which brings me back to the hours before my make-or-break performance at Constitution Hall in Washington, D.C., after I bombed in St. Louis and Cleveland. I had allowed my ego to consume my natural instincts and abilities to make people laugh. My career was in a tailspin and my future as a stand-up comedian was very much in doubt.

I had decided in the car on the way to the theater that if I bombed that night, it would be my last performance as a stand-up. In fact, I was so distraught I was prepared to quit show business entirely.

That was my frame of mind when I entered the venue and they told me that there was a very famous comedian waiting to speak with me in my dressing room. That comedian was my friend Martin Lawrence.

Hearing that Martin was there that night—the night I was convinced I was doomed to fail for the final time onstage—just intensified the pressure tenfold. I had tremendous respect for Martin's talent and I was horrified that he would be there to watch me go down in flames. I felt like a lamb headed to the slaughter. I was feeling really, really fucking paranoid.

I entered my dressing room and there was Martin.

"Hey, Charlie. How you feeling?"

Because I was so convinced I was destined to bomb that night, and that Martin was going to see it, I decided the only way to soften the blow was to warn the brother before it happened.

I said, "To be frank with you, Martin, things haven't been going quite right for me lately. I've been standing up in front of Mike Epps's all-black audiences, and they don't like me. They're angry at me. They're booing me off the stage, man."

Martin said, "Well, watchoo be sayin' to them?"

I began to describe my act. Martin interrupted and said, "No, what do you say to them first? You can't just come out and go right into telling jokes. You need to give the audience their props; compliment them. Break the ice by saying something nice about the city. Tell the ladies they look lovely and thank everyone for going to all the trouble of coming out to see you. Their presence is a gift to you, so be sure to return it. Start by introducing yourself to them. Shake hands first, and get them on your side."

Aha!

I had seen this happen hundreds of times, but I had never thought of it as a technique. If you go to any show—especially one with a one hundred percent black audience—the first thing a good comedian does is ingratiate himself with the crowd. In front of a mixed audience, for whatever reason, I was getting away with not doing that. With an all-black audience, I couldn't get away with it, especially since I was some new dude who they needed to warm up to and decide whether or not to bother giving me a chance. They knew my brother, but they needed to be introduced to me. And it was my responsibility to initiate that introduction.

I didn't know.

Martin said, "All you gotta do is go out there and ask everybody, 'How you feeling? You having a good time?' Compliment them first. When you come out and do that, when you plug in and tell them, 'Hey, you and I are on the same side; I think the world is fucked up, too,' they will listen to your jokes."

Once Martin explained it to me, I instantly realized that—for that night, and every night after—things were going to be all right. Going out onstage and refusing to shake hands first—forgetting to acknowledge the audience and be grateful for their participation in the performance—came off as pompous. It was easy for them to take one look at me with my sunglasses, fancy clothes, and jewelry, and say, "Fuck you, Charlie Murphy. Mr. Big Shot Eddie's brother. We don't even want to try to like you. You're not worth the effort."

Lesson learned.

I went out onstage that night in Constitution Hall and followed Martin's advice to make that all-important first connection with the audience, and I had a great show. And another great show after that. And soon after, in the fall of 2006, I was on the road with John Heffron and Joe Rogan for the "Real Men of Comedy" tour: twenty cities in thirty days.

Martin's advice was what I desperately needed to hear, and absorb, at a critical moment in my stand-up career. I had made the mistake of approaching my show like a rapper or singer whose stage presence is all about creating a certain mystique. The whole idea that the more glitter I wore (hadn't I learned anything from that busboy jacket?) and the more aloof I was with an audience, the more interesting I would be and the more they would be forced to respect me was off the mark. My thinking could not have been more misguided. A comedian can't be aloof. He's a man of the people, and he needs to be fully engaged with his audience, on their level. I had to learn to convey to the audience that we were cool with each other, like best friends.

By taking the time to stop by my dressing room that night in D.C., and making the effort to talk me down from the ledge, Martin Lawrence saved my stand-up comedy career. Because that was the very night I was ready to say "I quit."

But instead, I began a whole new life.

On stage at The Improv, 2008.

CHAPTER NINE

A STAND-UP GUY

When I look back at the span of my life, I see that doing stand-up comedy has been the most productive and creative period of my professional career. I don't work for anyone but myself, no one writes my show for me, and no one is onstage with me sharing the credit or the responsibility. I have finally discovered a talent that's *all me.*

Doing something entirely for myself is a new concept. In the Navy, everything was about the unit. No one person was more important than the group. Later, when I was rolling with Eddie as his head of security, it was still all about the group—banding together to keep Eddie, and one another, safe. After that, when I got into music production and several other endeavors in the entertainment field, again, it was all about the unit, not about the individual. Even screenwriting, which can be a lonely and isolating vocation, becomes a massive group undertaking and, regardless of how well your script is crafted, studio executives and everyone else with an opinion—from the star of the picture to the guy who services the watercoolers—will try to have a crack at rewriting your work. Before stand-up, decisions in my life were always made for the benefit of the group.

Now it's just me and a microphone.

I suppose one could argue that even stand-up is a group activity because it requires an audience to respond to the material—favorably or not. There's some merit to that, and I try to bring everything I have to each interaction I have with an audience.

To that end, I find that stand-up requires a lot of preparation. Some people think I just walk up onstage and folks start laughing, but it doesn't work like that. I have to earn every laugh I get.

When I prepare my material, I need time to be alone, especially when I'm getting ready to take the stage. I'm not very talkative for the few hours leading up to a performance. I don't really want to be around other people. There's a mental process that needs to happen for me to prepare for an audience. I need a quiet, calm environment. I don't want to allow any thoughts into my head about what's on other people's agendas; I just want to be alone.

I start by replaying what I did the last time I performed, focusing on what worked and trying to expand on it. I say my prayers beforehand because I believe that stand-up comedy is a spiritual exchange between the audience and me. People come to my shows with whatever problems are weighing them down, and my job is to make them laugh. I'm there to make them forget about whatever issues are plaguing them during that hour they spend with me. And together we keep a positive energy alive in the room.

I write down my set list over and over until I know it backward and forward. I constantly add and subtract material, study it, and focus on it for hours, until I'm confident in what I'm going to share.

At my shows, I set up a camera to record my performances. Like a cleanup hitter breaking down the film of each at-bat, I study every show closely to figure out where I can make improvements, and I use my "game" films to mark my progress over the years. I try to enhance whatever natural talent I have while shedding other, more amateurish behavior.

I draw my material from all sorts of resources. I watch and read the news every day, but I also make a point of reading all the garbage publications, too—supermarket tabloids and so forth. I try to listen to what people are talking about. Then I get my ass outside to experience things and talk with people face-to-face. I can't just sit around on the couch, waiting for inspiration to strike. Then I test out my new material during live shows by mixing it in with my usual set. That way, if a joke doesn't work or falls flat, I just move right on to one that I'm already confident will get a laugh.

Some people may disagree with me, but I believe that one

thing a good comedian does not suffer from is depression. A good comedian is out engaging with the world; a depressed dude is sitting at home in his underpants with the shades drawn, doing nothing. You know a great comedian just by looking at him—he's a vibrant force, glowing like a star at the center of his own universe, and you can't stop looking at him.

When I was writing only screenplays, all the jokes I came up with were played out solely in my head and set down on paper—never delivered to a live audience. I have seen my material translate from the page to the screen in movies and listened to the laughter in theaters from words I've written while sitting alone in front of my computer. Those experiences fooled me into believing that writing jokes for a stand-up act would be a breeze.

Wrong.

Of course, what I wasn't taking into account were all the things that go into the making of a movie that help get that big laugh: the other actors in the scene reacting to the joke, the lighting, the wardrobe, the setting, the sound track, and the special effects—all that and more contribute to producing a big movie laugh. It ain't just the words I wrote on the paper. Something may read funny, but it takes a special talent and skill to make it come off funny in live action. When a comedian can connect the words from a piece of paper with the collective mind of a live audience—enough to force a woman into labor or make a man shit his pants—that's when you've arrived in another comedy zone. When a comedian learns how to verbalize humor from the page to that effect, that's when he's learned the art of stand-up.

For me, comedy is of the moment. When I'm delivering my set, I feed off the energy of the audience. If I notice something going on in the crowd, or if I have a new thought, I might head off in a whole new direction. Sometimes it might only be a one-word spin on a well-worn joke, and suddenly it takes off like a dynamo. When I make that kind of connection with an audience, it helps me get a better feel for their sensibility. I'm able to gauge how I need to adjust my act to get a good reaction from them. Since *Chappelle's Show*, I tend to draw a very diverse audience, so early in my set I try some jokes to figure out what a particular audience is all about—then I hammer on the material that fits their humor. With some adjustments, my set does stay fairly constant, which is a testament, I hope, to how hard I work to cross boundaries and keep things fresh from multiple perspectives.

When I first started traveling the country for my live shows, I would try to schedule as many performances in a weekend as I could. After a while I realized I was missing out on the fun of seeing the places I was visiting, walking around, meeting people, and enjoying new experiences—all very important when it comes to writing material. I think part of my responsibility as a comedian is to meet as many people and listen to as many conversations, stories, and opinions as I can.

Comedy is all about observing everyday life and extracting the funny from it. When I started performing stand-up, I was booking four shows a night, and that was just too much. Now, at maximum, I do six shows total over a weekend. I try to come into town on a Thursday, do my show that night, and wake up the next day rested enough to check out the sights.

I've taken my kids along to my live shows before, but it's not really that fun. When I'm doing a show, each night's performance commands my focus for the entire weekend. That means during the daytime, I want to focus on me—getting sleep and relaxing in a quiet mind-set. I'm definitely not getting that when I bring my kids along; they are balls of energy and demand my full attention. When I'm with them, I have to be up and about, taking them out to experience things and keeping them occupied. The trade-off is that when my show rolls around that night I'm tired and not at the top of my game. So nowadays, for the most part, the little Murphys stay at home.

One casualty of my new lifestyle has been my parrot of twenty years, Madison. I loved that bird like one of my children. Birds are very social creatures, and Madison and I regularly spent many hours together before I hit the road for my stand-up. I didn't realize the effect my absence would have on him, and he died of loneliness and a broken heart. I realized too late that I should have taken him on the road with me. I cried like a baby when he died. I'll never get another bird as long as I live; I don't feel I deserve to be a bird owner.

Like every professional comedian, I have definitely had my share of odd encounters on the road. At a show in Omaha, Nebraska, I was performing in a gigantic bar where the owners made a stage by pushing together a bunch of tables. I was standing up on top of these tables, doing my show, and all through my act people from the audience kept coming up and placing shots of liquor in front of me. After a while, there were about fifty shots at my feet.

People were calling out, "Drink up, Charlie! Drink up!"

I said, "Yo, I would be dead if I drank all this booze."

Then somebody came up to me, stuck out his hand to shake mine, and put a fat bud of weed in my palm. It was good stuff, too. So I showed the weed to the crowd and they all started cheering, whooping, and hollering.

After my set I climbed down from the table-stage and started mingling with the crowd. One dude, slipping something into my hand, said, "Charlie, we want you to know how we all feel about you here in Omaha."

I could feel the object in my hand and—after kickin' it in the 1980s—thought it was a cylinder of cocaine. I was thinking, *These cats are really loose out here—one guy gives me weed, another hands me cocaine. . . .* I stepped into my dressing room, looked in my hand, and realized I had been handed a loaded

.30-06 shotgun round. A fucking bullet! So *that's* how they felt about me that night in Omaha? I left very quickly after that.

One of the stranger encounters I had on the road was when I was performing a show in Odessa, Texas. The comedy club was rented out for a show only once every other month. I didn't know that at the time; I thought it was all aboveboard. When I arrived, I noticed that the dude hadn't even cleaned up from the last time he'd done a show. There were two-month-old dishes in the kitchen, and dirt and dust lay over everything. The dressing room was just one couch with a curtain as the door. A Mexican comedian I had never met before came into the room. He started talking real fast and had a lot of game.

While he was talking, the curtain of our dressing room started moving in waves, like a storm was gathering on the other side. Suddenly a black dude with a head like a rottweiler stuck his face in and looked at the Mexican. Mind you, Odessa, Texas, is just a short walk across the border from Juárez, Mexico. Everybody in the audience was Mexican. The only two black guys in that entire venue were that rottweiler-faced dude and me.

Rottweiler said, "Come out here, Mexi*caaan*," really stretching out that last syllable.

"You gonna pay my money today, boy. That's right. You gonna pay it all. Or else somethin' gonna happen to you to-night. You gonna pay my money, *Mexican*." Then he popped his head back out of the curtain.

I was like, "Yo! Who the fuck was that guy?"

"Eh, it's this guy, man," said the comedian. "Says I owe him money. He keeps coming around, saying he's gonna fuck with me."

I said, "Man, you can't have dudes bursting into the dressing room with that kind of energy. You have to go out there and handle that shit."

"Oh, no, no, no. If I go out there, he'll pop me."

"Pop you?! Now you're definitely goin' out there, 'cause he ain't poppin' you in here, motherfucker. There ain't no room for poppin'. You have to leave. Now."

The curtain opened again. Rottweiler stuck in his head, saying, "Come on out here, Mexican. I'm waiting for you. COME ON OUT!"

The comedian said, "Look, I gave the money to your brother, man. I paid you already."

"Oh, really?" said Rottweiler. "You gave it to my brother?" He threw open the curtain. Standing beside him were four angry Mexican dudes, their muscles rippling. "Which one?"

It wasn't my problem, but I thought it was weird that four Mexicans had hired a black dude to get their money for them. Again I told the guy, "Yo, you gotta get out, man. This is too much."

The Mexican left and then came back after a little while, looking perfectly normal. The show went on that night without any incident. When it was over, he and I were sitting at the bar talking. He said, "I apologize for earlier, those guys coming in the dressing room. I got a little debt I gotta pay off. Don't take those guys seriously. That dude is always trying to seem tough. I mean, the last time he knocked me out—"

"Knocked you out? Whaddya mean the last time he knocked you out?"

"Oh, well, it's no big deal. And anyway, my hands were in my pockets."

I don't feel like I left Odessa, Texas, that night so much as I survived it.

I count that as one of my stranger experiences because my fellow comedians are never a source of trouble on the road. Before and after the shows, we hang together in the greenroom, go out to clubs, or grab a bite to eat—we're like a tight fraternity with a protective streak. But don't get me wrong; it's a competitive environment, with everyone jockeying for the same slots, bigger audiences, and better-paying gigs. That friendly spirit of competition traditionally doesn't include rottweiler-faced dudes showing up before the show to thump one of the performers (shit like that can seriously inhibit your mental preparation). But sometimes a rowdy audience member does want to charge the stage and thump you—and that can lead to some interesting interactions.

In Chicago, I had to deal with a heckler who kept disrupting my act. To make matters worse, I was hungover. This was before I learned my lesson about properly preparing both mentally and physically before a performance. I used to go out on the Thursday night I rolled into town and start drinking before my show.

What I didn't take into account was that Friday morning I had to be up at five o'clock to do radio promotion and interviews.

Before the Chicago show, I didn't go to bed all night, did my radio spots in the morning, and dragged my dead-tired ass back to my hotel room at about eleven o'clock. I couldn't get to sleep in the daylight so I just lay in bed, tossing and turning, and by the time I took the stage that night I was completely burnt out.

I was running on fumes when this guy down front started giving me a hard time. I don't wear my prescription glasses on-stage, so when I looked down into the crowd all I saw were two giant blurs in Chicago Bears jerseys. I saw this dude reaching over, hugging his big, mountain-sized man-lover.

I said, "You mean to tell me you wanna interrupt my performance all night and then act like I don't see you here in the front row, snuggling up to this big hairy dude next to you?"

"Goddamn it!" he yelled. "You're talking about my wife!"

The crowd started screaming with laughter.

I said, "Oh, man, I didn't mean to disrespect your wife. But I thought she was a man."

The crowd roared louder; they came unhinged. That's when the dude went fucking crazy and rushed the stage. He started pulling off his "Refrigerator" Perry jersey, screaming, "I'm gonna kill you!"

I said, "C'mon up here, if that's what you want. We can fight. But look, man, let me put it to you like this: Comedy and tragedy are related. People came here for a show. If they can't have laughs, your girlish screams will have to do. If I can't give them comedy, I'll give them your tragedy." I looked at the security guards holding him back and said, "Let him go."

They let him go.

The dude thought for a moment, then smiled and said, "I love you, Charlie Murphy."

"I love you, too, nigger. Now sit your fat ass down."

After my ego got the best of me on tour with Mike Epps, I started paying close attention to my appearance onstage, working to develop a style that was more muted. These days I lean toward a more raggedy look onstage, and I try to keep it real. I've developed a look that seems to connect with audiences, young and old, and keeps us on the same level so nothing distracts from my material. I leave the diamonds and gold at home now, and wear all silver. It looks nice, but nobody is focused on it during my performance, thinking, *Look at the size of the rock in that ring that asshole is wearing. I could send my kid to private school with that thing.* I don't want anybody thinking those thoughts while I'm trying to make them laugh. I don't try to impress anybody with anything but my comedy. I just try to be funny. And I always say my prayers before I go onstage. I've never had a problem again since that night Martin Lawrence opened my eyes to what I was doing wrong.

Speaking of personal style, one of my favorite comedians is

Tracy Morgan. I was in San Francisco once doing radio promotion for my weekend show when they told me Tracy was in the next studio.

I went over and Tracy said, "Yo, Charlie, c'mon in. Hey, this is my man C-Rock, in the house from New York." All in that voice that only Tracy can do.

We did an interview together, and all the while I couldn't stop staring at Tracy. I kept thinking, *What the fuck is that brother wearing?* Then it dawned on me: Tracy was wearing just a dirty white long-john onesie—the kind with the button-fold back door like they wore on *Gunsmoke*—and a pair of Timberlands. He was doing radio interviews in his drawers with all his jewelry on, and everyone acted as though he was dressed perfectly normal.

Since those early bombs in St. Louis and Cleveland rocked me to my core, I've learned many techniques to evaluate any weird energy I feel coming off the audience. I now know how to better navigate around potential problems much better than telling everyone to go fuck themselves, then dropping the mic and storming offstage.

I've walked into rooms since then and felt a similar vibe— that energy where the audience is looking at me critically, wondering what I'm capable of delivering. I think we've all felt

that energy before in our lives. I just didn't have the sophistica-
tion in my repertoire at the beginning of my stand-up career to
navigate around it. I knew that once I was able to master that
ability onstage, I would really be able to call myself a stand-up
comedian.

Today I tell young comedians, "It's okay to cry; just don't cry
in front of the audience. It's okay to sweat, but never let them
see you sweat. You're gonna cry and you're gonna sweat—just
don't do it in front of them. Don't ever let them know they
beat you."

The energy created in the room during a comedy performance is a very real thing. I believe that when I'm in the comedy
clubs, I can actually smell the energy in the room. I've come to
believe it's the phenomenon of a large group of people releasing
their pheromones into the air. There's a group thing happening
when people laugh and feel joy all together in one space. I think,
over time, that laughter and good energy build up, giving each
club its own unique scent. And it's always a good smell. That is,
unless some dude shits himself from laughing too hard.

That's why I don't tolerate hecklers, and why I don't treat
them with kid gloves. I think they spoil everyone else's good
time, and sometimes I'll have them thrown out of the club. But
distractions from the audience aren't always intended with mal-
ice. I did a live show recently where everything was going great
until I heard this dude call out, "Eddie Murphy's brother, you
sure are funny."

He did it during a lull when I wasn't talking, so everybody in the audience heard him say it.

I said, "Thanks a lot, man. Eddie Murphy's brother, huh? You must have just got home from prison. People don't call me Eddie Murphy's brother no more. That's what they used to call me when you went to jail. You must've been gone, what, ten years? Now people just call me Charlie Murphy."

That's the sort of comeback I have to be ready with to remind people that I'm out here doing my own thing and that they should judge that on its merits. Some people ask me why I even bother to respond to stuff like that. I say I do it because I can—and besides, it's fun. If somebody tries to take me down a peg, I'm glad I have the forum to respond. It's like I'm blowing a whistle and saying to them, "You committed a foul, asshole." I just try to play the game in a way that's always funny.

My stand-up now takes me overseas and up to Alaska and Canada. In 2007 I did two shows in Stockholm, Sweden. It was an experiment because every time I brought up the idea of taking my show to foreign countries, the issue of language barriers would always come up. The promoters were worried that the sensibilities were too different and that I would deliver too much material that people just didn't get. I started to buy into that way of thinking, too. But I told them straight up that the worst thing that could happen was that they wouldn't like me, and I wasn't afraid of that. So I kept beating the drum until they sent me over.

The whole idea of a language barrier is one of the great myths about performing abroad. The real deal on European audiences is that not only do they speak English, everybody in the crowd speaks, like, five languages. There's no need to worry about the audience not getting your act because—I got news for you—they're smarter than you are.

All that concern about language barriers turned out to be bullshit because I sold out and got standing ovations at every show. That got the promoters excited, so they had me back over in November and December of the following year for a fifteen-city tour of Scandinavia. I played stops in Sweden, then traveled on to Helsinki, Finland, and Copenhagen, Denmark.

Traveling around between shows, we had a female comedian with us named Beth Payne, who had to stop and go to the bathroom every twenty minutes. That transformed our four-hour ride into a five-and-a-half-hour one. The real burden of that situation was on my traveling companions, though, because you don't want to be in a car with me for that many hours. I'm talking and laughing the whole time. I don't let anybody go to sleep. It's torture.

As I explored Stockholm and Copenhagen, I found that they were definitely the kinds of cities that made me think, *I could live here.* Places with all the amenities of home, just with a different twist—those are the cities that pass the test for me. I don't recall having one bad experience in Europe, or meeting one negative person. The people were all very respectful and friendly. Not one person approached me on the street and demanded that their wife show me her titties. I'm not saying that shit doesn't happen in Europe, I'm just saying it hasn't happened to me so far.

When I returned from Scandinavia, I pushed to go on a five-city tour of Canada and to perform in Hawaii and Alaska. I pushed for all those shows because, as a comedian, there's such a thing as getting too comfortable. You can be on a circuit where you never leave your comfort zone and never stretch yourself to try new things. I'm not afraid to go anywhere. I say, "Send me to Iceland, send me to fucking Mongolia."

The process of getting up every week, putting my stuff together, and getting on a plane to go to another city is exciting. I think, *Man, I've been to Miami eight times now*, or *I've been to San Francisco six times now.* Whenever I go to these cities—or Houston or Boston or Copenhagen or wherever—it feels like I'm going home because I've been there so many times. When I'm in those places now, I know how to get around, where to go to relax, to see the sights, to eat a good meal. It's a different kind of satisfaction.

The best part of traveling is that everywhere I go I interact with people in airport terminals, on planes, in restaurants, in clubs, and on the street. I feel very fortunate because I've never had a negative or kooky person approach me (knock on wood). It's been all about the love. When people come up to me, I see them start to smile. I think they're smiling because they see me smiling. I've always been smiling. Even when I was a kid growing up in Brooklyn, Mom was like, "Y'know what, Charlie? Even when you be fightin', you be smilin'. You're even happy just to be fightin'."

It's just the way I am. Even when I relax my face muscles, I'm smiling. It's just how I was made.

In addition to traveling overseas in 2007, I filmed *A Perfect Holiday*, directed by Lance Rivera, which I think features some of my strongest work to date as an actor. I've never had the opportunity to play a character with as many different dimensions as I did in *A Perfect Holiday*. Lance really encouraged me to stretch in that film. He got me to do things I didn't know I was capable of as an actor. He even got Charlie Murphy to sing!

Lance was able to get me to understand my character's purpose for singing in that scene and what it brought to the story as a whole—so I did it. And he was right. Katt Williams and I had some really funny scenes together. I also got to work with Morris Chestnut, Gabrielle Union, and Faizon Love in that film, which was released in time for the following Christmas season.

The same year, I was thrilled to see the release of a major motion picture I cowrote with Eddie that has since grossed more than three hundred million dollars.

Norbit began as Eddie's idea. We were watching a video on the Internet about a man who was the victim of spousal abuse by his wife. They were out in the street, fistfighting Ali/Frazier–style, and she was beating him down. We thought that was off the chain and, apparently, women seemed to think it was funny, too. So we decided to write a movie about it.

At the time, I was headed up to Canada to shoot *King's Ransom* for New Line Cinema and I had exactly twenty-three days from the moment we decided to write *Norbit* to the day I had to arrive on set.

Eddie said, "I want you to write this movie. Check into a hotel and get it done." To turn the dial up on the pressure, he came back into the room, handed me an envelope full of cash, and said, "Here's your first payment."

Now there was no saying I was tired or couldn't come up with any bright ideas. I had to go to a hotel room, close the blinds, unplug the clock, phone, and TV, knuckle down, and start hammering out a story. I make it a habit to check into hotel rooms whenever I set out to write. I can't be around my normal environment—I can't have any distractions from family or friends. It's hard-core, but it's the only way I can get the work done. When it comes to writing, it always seems that there's nothing more important than having peace and quiet and sitting down in front of the computer screen to create something from your imagination. But I'm not picky about my space—any hotel will do.

If you want to be a writer, you've got to write day in and day out. That's the only way to learn your craft and to achieve your goals. I always write first in longhand and then type my work into the computer using a script-formatting software called Final Draft. For *Norbit*, I would mostly write all night and then show the pages to Eddie the next day. It's hard to describe how many stacks of paper I saw tossed in the garbage—twenty-five, thirty pages at a time. It was draining. The whole experience was a chore, a really grueling process. On the very last day before I caught my plane to Vancouver, I stayed up working for twenty-four hours straight. I delivered the first draft on a Friday; Eddie read it and said, "This is exactly what we wanted."

Feeling pretty good about that, I jumped in a car and drove straight to the airport.

On Monday Eddie called and said, "Guess what? Steven Spielberg read *Norbit*, and DreamWorks is going to produce it. Spielberg said that this is a great movie and he wants to do it right away."

I could not comprehend that I, Charlie Murphy, was being told on the phone that Steven Spielberg had just read the script I'd finished writing only three days earlier, that he loved it, and that he wanted to produce it.

What?

I was buggin'. That was one of the most energizing moments of my career. The thing is, when a writer submits a screenplay to be read, a guy like Steven Spielberg doesn't read it himself. He has an army of readers below him whose job it is to read for him and screen the material that goes forward. Then those readers send the best scripts up to their bosses, who are higher up in the production process. If they think the material is good, they send it on to Steven Spielberg. Maybe. So, for him to call back with that sort of enthusiasm in three days was fucking remarkable.

Eddie wasn't lying—DreamWorks *did* make it, with, like, a sixty-million-dollar budget. If I never write another movie again, I can always point to *Norbit*. That movie is on TV all the time now, and I feel a real sense of accomplishment when I see it and know that something that sprang from my head has touched so many people.

Writing is a part of everything I do these days. That's why I've created *Charlie Murphy's Crash Comedy* online on the Crackle Network. That material is going to be up on the Web forever; you don't get canceled from the Web. I look at that show as the opportunity to prove that I can create funny sketch comedy in my own style.

After I crossed paths with Freez Luv for the second time in 1995 on the set of the video *Murder Was the Case* with Snoop Dogg, we became close friends, and he now opens all of my shows.

When I think about all the years that have passed since we

met and all the characters who have surfaced and vanished in all aspects of the entertainment game, the fact that we can still be working, be relevant, and be friends means a lot to me.

Freez and I met up a third time when he moved from L.A. to Brooklyn. I had a bunch of shows lined up and asked him if he wanted to try to sit down together and write some material. Freez has been my opening act ever since. He gets the crowd going crazy and laughing hard before I come out. Freez is like my lead blocker: He goes out front and opens up a hole, and I run through for the touchdown. It's a true team effort.

You need a certain chemistry to collaborate on writing projects with a partner. It's hard to find a relationship where ego isn't the main issue to overcome (and I've certainly had my own epic battles against the power of the ego). In a bad situation, it usually starts when one guys says, "Well, my voice has to sound like this . . ." And it just gets worse from there. When that's the vibe, it doesn't take too long for the partnership to end. Freez Luv and I know each other's comic rhythms and we've learned how to coax the best material out of each other.

Ever since I was a kid I have been searching for an inner fire to ignite my passion and define my purpose in life—maybe even taking some cold comfort in half-believing that I'd never find it. After all, being somebody most folks have never heard of is easy, and it's made even easier when you spend a big part of your life standing next to a dude who's one of the most famous actors and comedians on the planet.

But I kept plugging away, trying a bunch of different stuff, and eventually I did get the breakout opportunity that all actors, writers, artists, and entertainers hope to garner one day through their efforts. I just hope I'm making the most of it.

My cousin, Rich, and me with the Tampa Bay Buccaneers, 2007.

CHAPTER TEN

"THAT'S WHAT'S UP"

Chappelle's Show catapulted me into a rare state of popular-ity and name recognition. But I had to take that opportunity, fig-ure out where I wanted it to lead, and then run with it, all while making adjustments on the fly. Chappelle's Show started me on this new career path, but I've had to figure out how to sustain it through a lot of trial and error, and by being humble and open to dealing with circumstances as they unfold.

Fame is a strange thing. There is an inexplicable aura sur-rounding it. With Rick James, I could actually see it pulsating all around him. There's no reason to react to famous people any differently than to anyone else—after all, famous people are just people. And yet something happens when we have that split sec-ond of opportunity to engage a person whom we have always admired from afar. It even happens to me. In fact, it just happened recently.

I was on a plane headed to L.A. I had my head down, reading a book, with my iPod's earbuds tucked in my ears. I looked across the aisle, and seated right next to me was Kareem Abdul-Jabbar. I sat there staring at him, hoping he would look over so I could wave and say "Hi."

The entire flight, not once did Kareem look at me.

The plane landed at LAX and I started thinking, *Now the dude* has *to look at me because we're getting off and we all need to stand up and get our luggage.*

To my amazement, Kareem reached up, opened the overhead bin, and pulled down his bag without needing to stand up. He did it all while seated and facing forward.

But instead of reading his body language and taking the hint that the dude was going out of his way to avoid eye contact and not interact with anyone on the plane, I stayed in my seat, staring at him, until all the other passengers had gone.

Kareem finally stood up. I jumped up behind him and, without any conscious signal carried from my brain to my hand, clutched his shoulder like an eagle's talons seizing its prey. I wasn't just touching his shoulder—I had a death grip on it.

In that moment, I had an out-of-body experience. I asked myself, *Charlie? What is your hand doing to Kareem Abdul-Jabbar's shoulder?*

Kareem looked at me and said, "Hey, man, what's your problem?"

"I don't have a problem. I just want you to know something."

"What?"

I didn't have anything to say. My mind was blank. After a long pause, I finally stammered, "They need you in L.A."

"What?"

Kareem turned and stormed off the plane like I was the biggest asshole he'd ever encountered. I just stood there alone in the aisle, thinking, *Wow. That was Kareem Abdul-Jabbar, man. Now he thinks I'm a fucking idiot.*

When Kareem turned to ask me what I wanted, I thought to myself, *Yeah, Charlie, what do you want? Why is it so important for you to detain Kareem Abdul-Jabbar on an airplane with your bullshit?*

The simple fact was, I was starstruck.

When I looked at Kareem, I was taken back in my psyche to when I was a little boy and he was still Lew Alcindor, who went on to dominate the NBA with his skyhook and his big afro.

That encounter with Kareem is a reminder to me today to always go easy on people when they approach me, screaming, "CharlieMurphaaay!" or when fans get nervous and do silly things like try to snatch off my glasses, or take my hat, or unzip my jacket for a picture, saying, "Show everybody your T-shirt, CharlieMurphaaay!"

I'm conscious of the fact that those people aren't necessarily assholes; they're just acting different because they've been momentarily thrown out of their comfort zone by the weirdness of fame—just like I was when I saw Kareem.

Since folks started gleefully screaming my name as one long word, I've had the opportunity to do endorsements for Boost Mobile, Budweiser, Sprint, Coca-Cola, and Nike, and I've done voice performances for *The Boondocks* and *Grand Theft Auto: San Andreas*. I never used to get those kinds of looks before from advertisers, shows, and casting directors. If you recall, I was elated that my first real acting gig was as a Jamaican assassin who gnawed off his own arm and then swam five hundred miles to freedom. But not much has changed since 1988—I was happy to get work then, and I'm happy to be working now.

I don't foresee any end to my love of doing stand-up comedy. It's not like I got famous for being handsome. I got famous for telling stories, then I took to the road to see if I could keep it going by telling jokes.

I'm no comedy expert by any means. I just try to improve every day. The only advice I will pass along to any young or aspiring comedians is this: You know, in your soul, that you're supposed to be up there onstage in front of that microphone. *You know it*. The audience knows it, too. Hold your ground and believe in your material. Believe in yourself.

As a stand-up comic, I hope I've earned a measure of legitimacy and originality with audiences. *Chappelle's Show* was hilarious and a great experience. I appreciate all the love and opportunity that have stemmed from that, but a couple of popular TV sketches were never going to make me legit as an entertainer—not in my mind, and not in anybody else's.

When I was red-eyed and exhausted, sitting in a subway car on my way home to Linden Street from McCarren Pool in Brooklyn; or when I was sitting in my cell in Nassau County Jail, serving hamburgers out from under my nuts; or when I was sweating my ass off in the belly of the USS *Joseph Hewes*; or when I was being swept up in a seemingly endless sea of joyous fans at a stadium show for my world-famous brother; or even as I sat, hunched over in a hotel room, tapping my feverish thoughts into my computer—I could never have imagined this life for myself. *Never.*

So that's what's up. I turn fifty this year and hope, with all sincerity, that I continue to connect with new fans along the way. In the end, I just want people to say, "Charlie Murphy? He's a funny dude. He does a great stand-up. And he's a real stand-up guy."

ACKNOWLEDGMENTS

Thank you to my family . . . my rock. Thanks to my team—you all know who you are. A huge thank-you to everyone who is a Charlie Murphy fan. Truly, without any of you, none of this would be possible. Last but not least, thanks to anyone who gets it and knows we were put here to be happy. Keep smiling and keep laughing. Just keep laughing! I feel blessed to be able to participate in an art form that allows even the insane to rise in its ranks. . . . May God bless all of you . . .